Ministering

With

Angels

By Paul David Harrison

Published by
Messengers of His Kingdom
P.O. Box 595351
Dallas, TX 75359
www.messengersofhiskingdom.com

Cover Art Work by Kent Robbins and Fabian Arroyo

Unless otherwise noted, scripture quotations are from the
HOLY BIBLE, Authorized King James Version.

Dedication

*To God, my heavenly Father,
for the passion He has put in me to seek His heart.*

*To Jesus Christ, Son of God, Chief Intercessor,
for the intercessory gifts He has given me.*

*To the Holy Spirit, my Comforter and Guide,
for revealing the ministry of angels to me.*

Table of Contents

Acknowledgements

First and foremost, this book is inspired by my precious Lord, who extended His mercy and grace and gave me a second chance. Thank you, Jesus.

To acknowledge all who have touched my life would be impossible. Thank you all, especially the leaders and members of Lakewood who have given their lives to serving the Lord with fervency I am continually astounded by.

There are others without whom this book would never have been written…

◊ My wonderful wife Joy who is truly my partner in ministry and to three of the dearest children in the world, Andrea, Aaron and April.

◊ Our parents, Don & Nelda Harrison and Wes & Karen Burns, who have loved, supported and prayed for us.

◊ Judy Vineyard, our beloved chief editor, who labored many hours teaching us the ways of book writing and kept the flatbread and coffee coming. Lana Bateman, Karen Burns, Jaine Burns and Carolee Welch who reviewed and proofed this book. Thank you for your friendship and this labor of love.

◊ The M.I.T. students who taught me more than I taught them. Thank you for trusting the Lord enough to step out in faith. Some of whose personal encounters with angels are recorded here.

◊ And finally, thank you to my dear friend and pastor, Ron Crawford. Your prayers, encouragement and covering have paved the way for this project. You have kept the faith and haven't lost your humor in spite of the incredible challenges we have had to face.

The Lord has truly blessed me by surrounding me with His intercessors and saints.

Thank you all.
Pastor Paul

Preface

Most Christians will readily attest to the fact that angels exist. The Bible is filled with examples of angelic activity and intervention on behalf of the people and work of God. When it comes to the subject of what angels are doing right now, there is an uneasy silence.

Paul Harrison brings to light the reality that angels are a very real entity, and that they are still very much in the framework of how God deals with His work and His people. **<u>Ministering With Angels</u>** is a most enlightening and insightful book on a subject of which the believer needs to know more. God has ordained a close relationship between His children and His angelic messengers in this hour.

The world is very much aware of the existence of the angelic. The stage for the revealing of the antichrist is rapidly being constructed, and thousands of people worldwide are being programmed with demonic doctrines and viewpoints regarding the things of the spirit realm.

However, a large segment of the church possesses a simple, perhaps even naïve viewpoint of the spirit world. This book is an eye opener to those who have believed the Bible, but have not known the power of the messengers that fill such a prominent role on its pages. No longer can the people of God afford to be blissfully ignorant. **<u>Ministering With Angels</u>** affords us the privilege of being better informed, and subsequently, better prepared for our task in these end times.

Allow me to offer a word of assurance regarding the author of this book. I have known Paul Harrison for well over a decade. He has served faithfully on my Pastoral Staff during that time.

If there ever was a man who exemplifies a standard for ministry, it is Paul. He was raised in a solid church environment, graduated from an accredited Bible college, served on a church staff while faithfully and lovingly raising a family. Truly this man has been known among us.

We often hear that it is wise to consider the source. Within our current world environment, especially in regard to issues surrounding angels and demons, it is of the utmost importance to consider your sources. Allow me the opportunity to validate this source. Paul Harrison loves God and is a man of constant intercession. He has been known among a reputable congregation of believers for many, many years.

We are at the end of the age. May you prayerfully and confidently consider the revelation and insights found within this book. You will need this information in the days that are upon us.

Senior Pastor
Ronald W. Crawford,
Lakewood Assembly of God,
Dallas, Texas

Introduction

WHY NOW?

"Blessed is *he that readeth, and they that hear the words of this prophecy, and keep those things which are written therein: for the time* is *at hand."*
-- Revelation 1:3

Christians today are living in the most exciting time in history. Our society has technological capabilities that boggle the mind. Life is moving at an accelerated pace. If you do not make the effort to learn and keep up with the e-world, you may find yourself scratching your head and wondering, "Why am I so far behind?"

These are the last days and the kingdom of God is being revealed exponentially. Many are receiving dreams and visions of coming events. The Holy Spirit is giving fresh revelations of the Word of God and greater insight into scripture that in the past were interpreted and taught with a limited scope of understanding.

I would like to share with you just one of the areas in which God, in His grace and mercy, is pulling back the veil and allowing us to see more clearly. This area of fresh revelation concerns the ministry of angels as they cooperate with born again believers to fulfill God's purposes on the earth.

There are many books that share incredible stories of angels saving lives and protecting people from potentially catastrophic events. This book takes a different look; a look at the angelic ministry God is making available to His children today. The events and revelations shared here align exactly with Biblical accounts of the angelic.

Our society is infatuated with angels. In fact, many recent Hollywood films explore the existence of angels and their interactions with man. Almost every night of the week, there are television shows that inaccurately depict the ministry of angels. This worldview is a deception directly from Satan. Satan is ahead of the church in explaining a supernatural reality, and he has skewed the truth for his own purposes. He has by far, the inside track over mankind on understanding the spirit realm. After all, Satan is a spirit and lives and operates in the spirit realm. Whereas, man's spirit is housed in a body and soul, living within the bounds of the physical realm. Satan knows the truth, but teaches a lie. Satan is a counterfeiter. He has taken things God created and perverted them.

God has purposed at this time in history to begin revealing many of the mysteries of His kingdom to the church. One of the mysteries of the spirit realm is His purpose for angels to minister with man. Remember what Jesus said in John 18:36, *"My kingdom is not of this world...my kingdom is not from hence."* Jesus' kingdom is spiritual and the mysteries of His kingdom are spiritual truths, many of which have been hidden until the end of time. The challenge, as God reveals these mysteries, is to set aside our preconceived ideas and allow God to stretch our faith.

This book is the result of my intense search for God. My search to know the truth and no longer be fooled by Satan's deceptions, and more importantly, my disgust with simply playing church, propelled me to seek God. As you will soon discover, when you purpose to find God's presence every day, His kingdom will come.

So, why another book on angels? Believe me, it was not part of my plan. I am simply obeying God. One day He directed me to "Put this revelation in a book." In the following pages, I have attempted to share what the Lord has revealed to me. Like the Apostle John was told in Revelation, "the time is at hand."

Chapter 1

THE TRANSFORMATION

"A new heart also will I give you, and a new spirit will I put within you: and I will take away the stony heart out of your flesh, and I will give you an heart of flesh."
-- Ezekiel 36:26

I once was a very ordinary Christian. I grew up in a wonderful Christian home where I was graciously sheltered from many evil influences. Church was always a part of my life. So, perhaps if you too are an "ordinary" Christian, you will understand that nothing in my upbringing prepared me for the encounters I am about to share.

Although I graduated from Bible college and have taken many post graduate courses, nothing I was taught prepared me to deal with what God was about to reveal. Quite by accident I discovered the reality of God. When I say the "reality of God," I am not talking about the reality that most are familiar with in traditional Christianity. I am talking about knowing God better than I know my wife, my family or myself. Walking daily in a place where His perspective is more important to me than anyone else's. Only God's perspective is important.

You see, God got a hold of me. Dear friend, what I want for you is to come into a place of knowing God, a place where God can get hold of you, too. The key is desperation. When I became desperate enough to pursue the reality of God's living presence in my life, my life took drastic turns. I learned that our lack of pursuit for God indicates how easily satisfied we are without the true reality of God in our lives. When we decide to go after God, He responds by coming hard after us.

> *"I cried unto the LORD with my voice, and he heard me out of his holy hill. Selah."*
> *-- Psalm 3:4*

> *"Draw nigh to God, and he will draw nigh to you. . ."*
> *-- James 4:8a*

If you are not desperate, what you are about to read may not have any positive effect on your spiritual quotient. On the other hand, if you are ready to give up everything -- and I mean everything -- get ready because God is going to help you make quantum leaps in your spiritual walk. Like the Apostle Paul on the road to Damascus, these leaps only come through a revelation from heaven.

> *"At midday, O king, I saw in the way a light from heaven, above the brightness of the sun, shining round about me and them which journeyed with me. And when we were all fallen to the earth, I heard a voice speaking unto me, and saying in the Hebrew tongue, Saul, Saul, why persecutest thou me? it is hard for thee to kick against the pricks. And I said, Who art thou, Lord? And he said, I am Jesus whom thou persecutest. But rise, and stand upon thy feet: for I have appeared unto thee for this purpose, to make thee a minister and a witness both of these things which thou hast seen, and of those things in the which I will appear unto thee;*

Delivering thee from the people, and from the Gentiles, unto whom now I send thee, To open their eyes, and to turn them from darkness to light, and from the power of Satan unto God, that they may receive forgiveness of sins, and inheritance among them which are sanctified by faith that is in me. "

-- *Acts 26:13-18*

God is unveiling many revelations in these last days. He is pulling out all stops, and opening up His kingdom as never before. He is making available to His children every possible resource. Why? To prepare the church for what lies ahead. First, I know the greatest days of the church are upon us and that millions of souls are going to be born into the kingdom of God -- born at an incredible rate. Second, the Lord wants to get the church prepared for the most vicious onslaught of demonic power this earth has ever experienced. Finally, I know that God will accomplish His purposes if men and women like you and me get in line with what He is doing. We can only do that when we know God and partner with Him for those purposes to be realized here on earth.

LET ME BEGIN MY STORY

Let me begin my story. God began asking me the question, "Who is your best friend?" At that time, it was a no-brainer. There was no other human being on this planet closer to me than my wife, Joy. We are one of those rare couples who were high school sweethearts, got married and stayed married. We love each other deeply. I know what you are thinking, "What about the Lord? Shouldn't He be number one?" I had to face the reality that the Lord was NOT my closest friend.

So, what would the answer be today? The answer, again, is a no-brainer. There is no question or hesitation. Now the Lord is my dearest friend. It is a friendship that is fueled by a passion to be in His presence every moment of every day. I am not talking about a cognitive realization of God; I am talking about an experiential relationship.

How did I get from there to here? I discovered prayer and intercession. I am addicted and they have become my life. I am consumed with God. My future is not my concern any longer. All my plans, dreams and hopes have been thrown aside. It does not matter what I want any more. Today, the only plans I have for the future are those that are revealed to me by the Holy Spirit. What might seem logical or appropriate in my thinking is not a consideration. I cannot live, nor do I want to live, without continually abiding and communing with the Lord.

Life no longer revolves around family or even ministry; it revolves around the Lord. God's priorities have become mine. No exceptions! Our family has made many adjustments to allow for this complete turnaround. My wife has had to get acquainted with a new man in her life. Homes, cars, material things and even future plans no longer hold any sway in our commitment. My passion is for the Lord. God is so faithful, when He changed me He brought my family along. Not only my wife, but also all three of our teenagers are seeking hard after God too. Remember the scripture promises,

> *"Therefore take no thought, saying, What shall we eat? or, What shall we drink? or, Wherewithal shall we be clothed? (For after all these things do the Gentiles seek:) for your heavenly Father knoweth that ye have need of all these things. But seek ye first the kingdom of God, and his righteousness; and all these things shall be added unto you."*
>
> *-- Matthew 6:31-33*

I was not the only one desperate for God; our senior pastor was just as desperate, maybe even more so than I was. It was contagious. Soon many in our congregation were seeking God with all their hearts, and God changed our church. Our church is no longer a group of individuals with different interests that just happen to worship together and then go our separate ways. We are a core group of disciples whose main focus in life is our devotion to our Lord Jesus Christ. We all have different occupations and life situations, but we are one. Maybe you are thinking, "I can serve God and not have God shake up my life." Please, if you do not hear anything else, hear this; if you want to have encounters with God and become one of His friends, your life will be shaken!

Most of the potentially best years of my life were wasted on SELF. I also wasted many years of ministry. My desire was to provide the best ministry possible for those I was serving, and I was one of the busiest ministers you could find. However, I had to learn the hard way that God is not looking for busy ministers, nor is He looking for employees. God is looking for intimate friends. It is all about getting to know Him.

What does this newfound intimacy with the Lord have to do with **Ministering with Angels**? It has everything to do with it. All the revelations our church and staff have been privileged to receive including the revelation of ministering with angels were born out of an ongoing intimate relationship with the Lord. It is ongoing corporate and individual intercession that fuels the changes and revelations God pours into lives. If we had not had the hunger and the passion for intimacy with God, we would not have been able to persevere to where we are at this present time. Revelation changes things.

The Lord began changing our church in 1996. In 2000, God specifically told us to begin sharing the process through which He has taken us and make known the revelations He has given us to the body of Christ. This book is the story of our journey through the events, lessons and revelations the Lord used to transform us. The things you will read come directly from prayer journals, reflecting my experiences and those of many in our congregation.

The things that have happened are merely by-products of worshipping, seeking and crying out to God. I never sought the experiences I am about to share. God in His mercy and sovereignty has chosen to reveal this part of His kingdom. I hope by sharing my testimony with you that you will see God can use anyone. He wants to use you.

Chapter 2

A TRIP TO PENSACOLA

"Because thou sayest, I am rich, and increased with goods, and have need of nothing; and knowest not that thou art wretched, and miserable, and poor, and blind, and naked: I counsel thee to buy of me gold tried in the fire, that thou mayest be rich; and white raiment, that thou mayest be clothed, and that the shame of thy nakedness do not appear; and anoint thine eyes with eyesalve, that thou mayest see. As many as I love, I rebuke and chasten: be zealous therefore, and repent."

-- Revelation 3:17-19

In September 1996, our senior pastor, Ron Crawford, told me that a couple in our church was paying the expense for the pastoral staff to attend a Minister's Conference at Brownsville Assembly of God in Pensacola, Florida. I had heard about some of the "strange" things that happened in that church and I was semi-curious but mostly critical. In fact, when I first heard about the "Brownsville Revival," I thought people were talking about the city of Brownsville, Texas. I had no clue.

Initially, I was not very excited about going. Actually my first thought was "How can I get out of this?" You must understand I was a

11

consummate critic of anything that might be deemed "spiritual." If God was going to do anything special, He could do it right here in Dallas. Why should I have to travel hundreds of miles when God was everywhere? After all, God is in our church, too!

Why should any one church be singled out for a special outpouring of God? God does not show favoritism, does He? What good is a revival anyway? People just make a fresh commitment to God, only to back out of it a couple of weeks later. My thinking was that we did not need people who were off-center in their experiences with God. We need people who are grounded in the Word, logically minded, and faithful to their church. For that matter, spiritual people are spooky! These thought patterns were the very foundation of the distorted way I reasoned through all spiritual things. As the trip grew closer, and I was unable to come up with a legitimate excuse, I realized I was going on this trip, like it or not.

In my opinion, if I thought something was not of God, that settled it for me. I just knew God would not operate or do anything outside of my own convictions. After all, He had put those convictions in my heart in the first place, right? I considered it my duty as a minister to be skeptical. I had convinced myself I was only acting in the best interest of God to protect God's people from becoming unbalanced.

Now, to set the stage, you will need to know a little more about me. I gave my heart to the Lord at the tender age of seven and never got into any serious trouble. I was faithful to God and to my church. I was baptized in the Holy Spirit with the evidence of speaking in tongues in my early teens. The Lord called me into the ministry during my teenage years, but after graduating from high school I opted to go to junior college and not Bible school. The Lord kept reminding me of my calling, but I kept putting Him off. To be honest, I did not want to go to Bible school, so I finally decided to compromise with God and become a psychologist instead. After a couple of years of study, I was miserable and I knew why.

I finally gave in and told God I would go into the ministry. So I changed my degree plan, wrote off a couple of years of psychology credits and went to Bible school, graduating in 1984. I worked as the children's and youth pastor at a great church in east Dallas from 1982-1987, where I learned the ropes of being a minister. In 1987, I joined the staff of The Father's Church (f/k/a Lakewood Assembly of God) under the newly elected senior pastor, Ron Crawford. Initially, I was the children's and youth pastor, later became the Minister of Education, and most currently, the Associate Pastor. Our congregation has been wonderful and incredibly supportive of my family and me.

As I look back, I realize that I was a negative and cynical person. I could not imagine anyone being a "better Christian" than me. What pride! This kind of prideful thought process did not bring me closer to God, but into a terrible state of lukewarmness.

Over the years I had developed a very lackadaisical attitude toward the spiritual disciplines of prayer and worship. A five-minute prayer a day was plenty for me and worship was no more than three hymns on a Sunday morning. Despite my own lack of spirituality, I was always first to assess someone else's spiritual state. I was much like the Pharisees and Sadducees who Jesus said could see clearly the inadequacies of others and yet were totally blind to their own shortcomings.

Ministering with Angels

Year after year I became more and more critical of other ministries and of our own congregational members. I had very little tolerance for failure in others, but gave myself a very wide margin for error. Consequently, this critical and religious spirit bled over into other areas of my life.

When you become critical and judgmental of others, there is a good chance there are sins and other issues lurking in your own life. In retrospect I can see clearly the pathway of my near destruction. I honestly did not see it then, but the Lord opened my blinded eyes.

Like so many people in church today, I needed to be entertained. I loved to watch movies. On my day off I would go see the latest movie showing at the theatre or rent a couple of videos. My discretion began to wane. Just as a drug addict must find something stronger to bring the next high, I had to have more shock and soon started watching R-rated movies. A double standard developed!

I could judge someone mixed up in pornography but did not think it wrong for me to watch an unclad woman in a movie. The scripture says in 1 Timothy 4:2, *"Speaking lies in hypocrisy; having their conscience seared with a hot iron;"* I would have denied all day long that this was the state of my heart, but it was true. I was lying to myself about what God expected of Christians. Like so many others, I made the Word fit my own desires and justified my actions with scripture instead of measuring them by scripture. I cannot tell you how close I came to becoming a reprobate.

So I grew more miserable by the day, finding myself getting angry for no apparent reason. I would blow up at my wife and children. You would think that a minister of the gospel would know better, and I really should have; however, at this point I was trapped. Lust, criticism, anger and discouragement had all wielded their way into my life and were getting out of control.

I was a Minister of Education. I was very active in my church and had grand plans and programs. To this day there are those who come and say, "I remember when you did this or that. What a wonderful ministry you developed." I was doing everything "right" BUT I was a backslider and deep down I knew it. How did I get myself into this predicament?

As the years quickly passed I found myself burned out with ministry life and started wondering if a sabbatical from the ministry might be a good idea. I have since learned that being burned out is a good indication of one's spiritual quotient. Sad to say, I think my quotient was near zero.

It was during this time of incredible frustration that the invitation to attend the revival in Pensacola, Florida came. It was God's perfect timing. During the weeks preceding the trip, the Lord began drawing me to Himself. I found myself going into our sanctuary to pray, which was very unusual for me. During one of these conversations with the Lord, I told the Lord I was tired of my hypocritical life and if something did not happen on this trip I was ready to walk away from the ministry. God began talking to me about starting over. I did not know you could do that. God was graciously preparing the soil of my heart. To my surprise, during those final days leading up to our trip, I was getting excited. I knew that one way or another, a decision would be made while I was there.

A FRESH PERSPECTIVE

On the second Tuesday of November 1996, three of us arrived in Pensacola, my senior pastor, Ron Crawford, our youth pastor and myself. We checked into our hotel, ate dinner and headed to the church. It was 7:00 p.m. when we arrived at Brownsville Assembly of God. The church was filled to capacity.

The atmosphere in the building was incredible, filled with great excitement and anticipation. The lights faded and the choir began singing "Lord Have Mercy" as prayer banners were brought out. My heart was melting fast as the anointing of the Lord began to penetrate. To my surprise, I was not feeling condemnation but the incredible warmth of the love of the Lord.

One might have thought the building was full of heathen instead of preachers that night. Evangelist Steve Hill did not pull any punches; he addressed our sins and told us we needed to repent. When the altar call came, under the conviction of the Holy Spirit, I made my way down to the front along with hundreds of others. My prayer that night was very simple, "God give me one more chance." This was not a simple rededication; it was more like I had been born again.

After the altar call, the Brownsville prayer teams were released to pray for people who wanted prayer. The man that prayed for me was very soft spoken. He put his fingers gently on my head, prayed and I quietly fell out in the Spirit.

On Wednesday, the second day of the conference, we attended several classes taught by the staff of Brownsville and other visiting ministers. That evening we were determined to get to the service early enough to sit where the river of God began flowing when the revival broke out on that glorious Father's Day in 1995[1]. We sat on folding chairs close enough to the stage to rest our feet on the steps. When the altar call came, those of us on folding chairs were asked to pick up their chairs and file to the back of the sanctuary. With the altar area being so crowded, we decided to return to our hotel, so we did not receive any individual prayer that night.

About 7:00 a.m. on Thursday morning I woke up with the presence of God all over me. As I lay in bed, God began speaking to my heart. I could hear Him so clearly. He asked if I would be willing to confess my sins to my pastor. I said, "Yes, I would." The Lord and I agreed that this confession would be done after we got back to Dallas. I cannot describe the huge burden that lifted off of me at that moment. The peace of knowing you are right with God is incredible.

A RUDE AWAKENING

As I sat up on the side of my bed, I noticed that one of my legs began to vibrate. This had never happened to me before. Not knowing what was happening, I tried stilling it with my hand, but to no avail. After a few moments, my other leg began vibrating. I figured the logical thing to do was to take a shower. Hopefully the warm water would relax my muscles and calm the shaking.

I made my way into the bathroom, got into the shower and turned on the water, waiting to see if the problem would correct itself. Instead of calming down, both of my legs began jerking violently. To keep from slipping and breaking my neck, I laid my whole body up against the shower wall. This too was to no avail. I now had a serious problem.

17

Ministering with Angels

After some time, I was miraculously able to get out of the shower and back to my bed.

To know me is to know a stubborn man. I was determined that this shaking was not going to beat me. Allow me to pause for a moment and point out our sleeping arrangements. The youth pastor and I were sharing a two-story loft. Pastor Crawford was in a separate room. I am sure you have already guessed it, my bed was on the second floor. Undaunted by my new handicap, I managed with great difficulty to get my pants on over my shaking legs and finish dressing. I was now set to attack the very steep staircase. Without knowing it, this may have been the first angelic assistance I received. I very gingerly made my way down the stairs and sat on the couch in the living room.

Still lying in his bed, probably wondering why I had made the entire racket upstairs, our youth pastor looked over and asked if I was okay. I said I was fine, but I could not get my legs to quit jerking. Back then one of my morning traditions was to drink a diet Dr. Pepper; I called it my morning coffee. So after a few minutes, I stumbled into the kitchen and grabbed a can of Dr. Pepper, pulled the tab, took a drink and sat the can on the counter. The moment the can touched the counter I was thrown backwards into the refrigerator door. I was literally thrown! At that time, I could not explain how.

The next several hours can be best characterized as violent. I felt like I was in a wrestling match, in which I was unable to defend myself. My body was twisted and contorted as I was thrown against the kitchen cabinets and rolled about on the floor. For the first time, I truly understood what Jacob must have felt like when he wrestled with the angel. I had absolutely no control over my body; my eyes were shut tight and my tongue locked. I could not see or speak. However, my ears were working just fine and I could hear the door shut as the youth pastor left. I was thinking, "Thanks! Just leave me here like this!" But, after a few minutes of watching me, the youth pastor had headed out to get Pastor Crawford. It was not long before I heard them come in. I still could not see or speak; but I could hear Pastor Crawford praying. It would be five-and-a-half hours before I was finally free to move under my own power again.

The events of that historic day have forever changed my life. The Lord spoke and did some incredible things in that hotel room. We experienced times of great laughter and times of intense prayer. There were some amazing prophetic proclamations, but most of all there was deliverance. It would be several months before I would finally realize what happened to me that day. What I can say is that before that day I had problems with lust, but afterwards it was gone! The critical spirit was gone and so was the religious spirit. God delivered me Himself that day! I now understand that God sent a couple of angels to wrestle off the demons I had unknowingly allowed in my life. They had attached themselves to me, but now, "What freedom!"

As you will read in the upcoming chapters, God also used the events of that day as a catalyst to bring new life to our congregation.

---

[1] **When the Heavens are Brass**, by Pastor John Kilpatrick, Destiny Image Publishers, Inc. 1996.

Chapter 3

A CALL TO PRAYER

"As many as I love, I rebuke and chasten: be zealous therefore, and repent. Behold, I stand at the door, and knock: if any man hear my voice, and open the door, I will come in to him, and will sup with him, and he with me. To him that overcometh will I grant to sit with me in my throne, even as I also overcame, and am set down with my Father in his throne."

-- Revelation 3:19-21

About two weeks after the Brownsville trip the Lord told my wife and I to sell our home and move closer to our church. Our home was in the country, situated on six-and-a-half beautiful acres about 35 minutes outside of Dallas. It was the perfect place to raise our three children, Andrea, Aaron and April. We had our own fishing pond, stables for horses, dog kennels and pasture enough to raise a few head of cattle. We even had our own baseball diamond, built for our son's little league team to practice on. Our children loved living in the country and so did we. We had just spent approximately $40,000 to completely remodel our home and planned on retiring there. But the Lord had different plans. He told us to move back into town and so we obeyed. Believe it or not, it was not a hard thing to do. As much as we loved our house and the plans we had made for our future, our hearts changed to embrace the Lord's command. We could not find a buyer quick enough.

One of the first major changes I felt immediately following our trip to Brownsville was a deep desire to pray. That was huge! Before this trip, I would normally pray about five minutes a day and that included praying for meals. Suddenly a deep hunger to spend time with the Lord became the center of my life. As a pastoral staff, we began to pray together for several hours each weekday morning before going to our offices. Additionally, within two weeks of our return we began gathering every Saturday evening for a couple of hours to pray as a congregation. This prayer time was dedicated to seeking God for our Sunday services. We also prayed for 30 minutes to an hour before and after both the morning and evening services on Sundays and Wednesdays. I am not saying this in pride; we were just hungry for God.

As this hunger to pray grew within me, I began praying with my understanding and in the Spirit. However, as I prayed in the Spirit, I became aware that my prayer language was expanding into multiple prayer languages. In fact, the more I prayed in the Spirit the more different languages I spoke. I would often speak in twenty or more languages during one session of prayer. This was a new experience for me, one that for many months I did not understand. I was not the only one experiencing this phenomenon, almost everyone that participated in prayer, noticed this same change and expansion in their prayer languages.

Remember how "busy" I had been? As I devoted myself to more prayer and as the weeks went by, the Lord began speaking to me about stepping away from many points of leadership responsibility in our church. He wanted me to focus on Him by spending even more time in prayer. God was putting me into His school. Pastor Crawford was in complete agreement with the transition the Lord was taking me through. At the Lord's direction, I started studying the Word and reading several books each week on the current move of God. I took many books out of my library to make room for these new authors, most of whom I had never heard of before. God miraculously brought me to scripture passages and godly writers with each new lesson in His school.

For the most part, we knew nothing as a church about intercession. In our ignorance we asked the Lord to teach us how to pray and He did! Many unusual things began happening in our prayer times. For example, frequently multiple intercessors would pray in the same unknown language, coincidentally most of our intercessors received the gift of divers tongues.

Another unusual experience was regular visitations by angels. It was not long before the Lord began showing Pastor Crawford, who had always had a seer's anointing, the most amazing things in the spirit realm. He began seeing an influx of angels during both our prayer times and worship services. Others in our congregation began seeing angels as well. On one such occasion, a Hispanic member brought a visiting pastor from Mexico (who did not speak English) to a Saturday prayer time. As he walked into our sanctuary, angels immediately greeted him. You should have seen his face... pure joy! He returned home to Mexico to tell his congregation and pastor friends about the angels he had seen. This was a confirmation to us that we were not just convincing ourselves or some type of "group think" was occurring. The Lord is good both to test our faith and to bring confirmation when we least expect it.

Ministering with Angels

The Lord taught me through the gift of discerning of spirits how to detect when an angel was standing near me. Although I could not see the angels, the Lord was teaching me to perceive or sense them. There were many times that Pastor Crawford told me, after prayer, that he saw an angel(s) standing over me on the very days when I had sensed their presence. At other times, I would ask Pastor Crawford if he had seen anything and his response aligned exactly with what I had perceived about an angel standing near me. These confirmations really helped to build my faith.

Our times of intercession were dramatically enhanced with the arrival of the angelic. Some might say it was just the anointing, and at face value I would agree. However, the anointing rests heavily on the angels and their interjection into prayer times has specific characteristics. For example, there is an increase in the number of languages being prayed, and strange sounds and noises are heard. I believe these noises to be echoes of heavenly sounds and activities. Often when the angels show up, the whole prayer group will feel an internal spiritual surge. There is an immediate increase in the volume and speed of the tongues, as well as an increase in the number of tongues spoken (divers tongues). For instance, the room can be completely silent during a time of prayer, with individuals scattered in different pews and locations in the sanctuary, praying independently of each other. Then suddenly everyone will erupt in loud prayer, singing or in wails of intercession. No one initiated this simultaneous eruption of passionate intercession and worship.

The angels also bring a powerful anointing for agreement in prayer. Amazing things happen as they enter into intercession with us. When the warring angels come, intercessors often react to their presence by dancing or moving their arms. There is generally a lot of singing in the Spirit when there are worshipping angels present.

Sometimes the arrival of angels will signify an imminent visitation of the Lord Jesus Christ. On many occasions the Lord sent His angels ahead to prepare us by anointing us and clothing our spirit man. Just like the father commanded his servants to put the best robe on his prodigal son.

> *"But the father said to his servants, Bring forth the best robe, and put it on him; and put a ring on his hand, and shoes on his feet: ..."*   -- *Luke 15:22*

> *"And I said, Let them* [angels] *set a fair mitre* [diadem] *upon his head. So they set a fair mitre upon his head, and clothed him with garments. And the angel of the LORD stood by."*
>   -- *Zechariah 3:5*

These times of being drawn into the presence of the Father on a one-on-one basis are some of the most personal and intense moments with God.

Dear friend, I am guessing you were reading along just fine until about two paragraphs ago. Now you are beginning to wonder. I can see the questions popping into your mind.

> *Do angels pray and intercede like people? Strange sounds, is that biblical? Divers tongues, isn't that when God miraculously gives a missionary a foreign language?*[1]

Bear with me, please. Trust in the Lord as you continue to read, and He will give you the answers to these questions and more.

---

[1] **God's Generals**, by Roberts Liardon, Albury Publishing, 1996. (pg. 156)

Chapter 4

DIVERS TONGUES

"To another the working of miracles; to another prophecy; to another discerning of spirits; to another divers kinds of tongues; to another the interpretation of tongues: ..."
-- 1 Corinthians 12:10

LET'S BE HONEST

Ninety-nine percent of the church has no concept of the gift of divers tongues or its purpose and function in the body of Christ. Many Pentecostals and Spirit-filled believers are taught about "speaking in tongues" as the "initial physical evidence" of the baptism in the Holy Spirit and not about the gift of divers tongues. Believers often neglect to pray and worship in the language given to them when they are baptized in the Holy Spirit. With this neglect and misunderstanding of the importance of speaking in tongues, it is no wonder there is so little understanding or teaching about the gift of divers tongues. Again, the prayer language one receives when baptized in the Holy Spirit IS NOT the same as the gift of divers tongues.

Fortunately, I had a mother who had no problem praying in the Spirit, out loud! I was always amazed at how the level of power and anointing increased when she prayed in the Spirit. Our family was also part of one of those unusual Pentecostal churches, which on occasion worshipped in tongues as a congregation. Very few of the Spirit-filled congregations I have visited have even this level of freedom in the Spirit.

Let's be honest. Speaking in tongues is not part of the daily regimen of most Spirit-filled believers. Personally, I was very negligent about praying, but especially about praying in tongues. When I did pray in tongues, my prayer language was very predictable. By that, I mean I knew what the language was going to sound like and even recognized a lot of the words, although I did not know what they meant.

Growing up I always understood "divers tongues" to be an additional language you received to speak forth a message in tongues during a service or, as mentioned earlier, it had to do with foreign missions. It was two days after our return from Pensacola that I noticed I was speaking in several new languages. These prayers were coming from deep within, not just out of my mouth. In studying the scriptures, I soon found that the abdomen is where the spirit of man dwells.

> *"The spirit of man is the candle of the LORD, searching all the inward parts of the belly."*
> *-- Proverbs 20:27*

> *"He that believeth on me, as the scripture hath said, out of his belly shall flow rivers of living water."*
> *-- John 7:38*

An amazing thing I discovered was that praying in the spirit in divers tongues is like flying on automatic pilot. The less I worked at praying, the more powerfully the Holy Spirit would rise up and pray through me.

The Holy Spirit was doing the work of intercession with little effort on my part. Although this new gifting enabled me to pray for hours at a time, my physical body was not accustomed to the power of the Holy Spirit surging through it. It was a total workout, but I loved it!

How did it work? I would lie on the floor and the anointing for intercession would come. For me, the anointing would come when I lay down. For others, their physical position did not seem to matter. The Lord told me months later that my lying down to pray was a prophetic stance associated with my personal calling. In any case, when I would lay down and begin praying in the Spirit, this turbo-charged anointing for intercession would come upon me.

This turbo-charged intercession is something to behold and more incredible to experience. Languages of every kind would start pouring rapidly out of my mouth. It is like being fluent in all these languages, speaking effortlessly hundreds of words and sentences. They are spoken forth boldly and with authority. My whole body quakes as the anointing for intercession grows and increases. It is not uncommon to see some people shake quite profoundly. The languages can have a Slavic, Oriental, French, Indian or other dialect sound to them. In the early days almost everyone was praying in what sounded like a Korean or Chinese dialect. It was not uncommon for an intercessor to pray in several different languages during their prayer times. The Apostle Paul began his famous chapter on love, 1 Corinthians 13, with the words, *"Though I speak with the tongues of men and of angels,"* we know the Apostle Paul prayed in divers tongues.

Most of our prayer times are corporate, although we also find places to pray alone. However, the "divers tongues gift" has incredible potency when two or more are flowing together. For example, many times several intercessors will be flowing in the same language (agreement power) at the same time. We have also experienced peaks and valleys during the prayer sessions. By that I mean it can be very quiet for awhile, with everyone praying totally independent of each other, and then suddenly a wave of anointing will hit several of us simultaneously and loud prayer will erupt. Then just as quickly, all will get quiet again. It's a miraculous thing to behold. The Spirit of the Lord magnificently orchestrates our prayers.

Jesus described how prayer should operate.

> *"Again I say unto you, That if two of you shall agree on earth as touching any thing that they shall ask, it shall be done for them of my Father which is in heaven."*
> *-- Matthew 18:19*

The word "agree" in the Greek is "*sumphoneo*." It means to be harmonious or to agree together. Pastor Crawford likens it to a symphony conductor bringing all the instruments together to form a harmonious, glorious sound. Much like a master composer bringing the melody and harmony together to form a beautiful piece of music. You cannot make this type of prayer happen, it is birthed and sustained by the Holy Spirit.

We simply asked the Lord to teach us to pray, and this is how He taught us. He instructed us to not pray for individual requests during our prayer times but to come into the sanctuary and find a place to pray and pray! We do not sit around and fellowship, when we come to pray and we do not spend our time telling each other our personal prayer requests. We get right to work and pray. We do not pray what we want; we pray what the Holy Spirit wants us to pray. People often write their personal prayer requests on a piece of paper, and our prayer team members pray for them outside of scheduled prayer times. We DO NOT interrupt the Holy Spirit directed times of prayer.

Our main focus in prayer is to touch the Father's heart with our worship and cry out for His purposes to be fulfilled on earth as it is in heaven. We have no other agendas in our prayer times. Once in a great while we might mention something that, as a church we need to be praying for, but a request like that is usually communicated during a church service and not in a prayer meeting.

What is extremely interesting is that when this gift is flowing, our spirits seem to communicate with one another. There are times when I know exactly who I am agreeing with in prayer, and we might even have a conversation in the Holy Spirit with one another. We have sung the song, "We are one in the Spirit, we are one in the Lord," but probably have not realized that praying together in the Holy Spirit is a powerful part of what that actually means.

The Holy Spirit has used the gift of divers tongues as an explosive weapon in intercession as well as in spiritual warfare. This gifting is a vehicle to communicate with the angels in their own language. This communication with angels has caused us to receive more revelations from the Heavenly Father and move with greater authority in the heavenlies. Divers tongues has also enabled us to deal with demons in a more effective way. We may not always understand what we say, but the Spirit of the Lord does. He always knows the right words to say.

> *"Likewise the Spirit also helpeth our infirmities: for we know not what we should pray for as we ought: but the Spirit itself maketh intercession for us with groanings which cannot be uttered."*
>
> *-- Romans 8:26*

We will talk more about how divers tongues has affected our ability to communicate with angels in the next chapter. For now, let us talk about how divers tongues can help you and your church in spiritual warfare and coming against opposition in prayer. I have had to face off with plenty of evil spirits. Demons or evil spirits are actually fallen angels. Like everything else in the demonic arena, their languages were once heavenly, but are now polluted and perverted as a result of their rebellion against God.

Utilizing the gift of divers tongues, the Holy Spirit through us will speak to the demons in their own language. Why would we want to do that, you may ask? When you have to face off with a demon in the spirit realm or in a deliverance situation, there is greater authority when you speak to them in their own language. You might not understand what you are saying to them, but you can be sure the Holy Spirit knows what needs to be said. There are times when the Holy Spirit will give us an interpretation of what is being said. Personally, I do not worry about it. All I know is that the enemy obeys the Holy Spirit that is speaking through me.

I believe as time goes along and we come to understand more about the divers tongues gifting, we will be amazed at how vital it is when dealing in the supernatural world. I can foresee deliverance ministries moving along much more rapidly. The Holy Spirit knows what needs to be done and can cut to the quick. In one situation where I was ministering deliverance, the person who was being delivered was filled with the Holy Spirit during the deliverance process. After a few moments I was communicating with their spirit about what was going on inside of them. This is not an easy process to explain on paper, but many of you may experience similar occurrences.

For greater insight into divers tongues, I would strongly recommend that you get Pastor Ron Crawford's newly released book on **Divers Tongues**. It can be obtained from Pneumatikos Publishing, P.O. Box 595351, Dallas, TX 75359 (214) 821-5290, www.pneumatikos.com.

Chapter 5

WELCOMING
THE ANGELS

*"And there arose a great cry: and the scribes that were of
the Pharisees' part arose, and strove, saying, We find no evil
in this man: but if a spirit or an angel hath spoken to him, let
us not fight against God."*

-- Acts 23:9

Angels began making their presence known during our prayer times
soon after our trip to Brownsville. Often the angels stood over me, and
at other times they talked to me. They brought messages from the Lord
and ministered His peace, love and comfort. They also brought
prophecies and fresh revelations from the Word. These wonderful
angelic visitations soon became an every day experience in which the
Lord poured many things that were very dear to His heart into mine. I
received many prophetic words about my life, our church, and the things
that will soon happen on this earth and in the heavens.

Human bodies often react to the presence of God's glory and power.
Angels definitely come clothed in the power and glory of God. One of

many scriptural examples is when Daniel lost all his strength in the presence of angels.

> *"For how can the servant of this my lord talk with this my lord? for as for me, straightway there remained no strength in me, neither is there breath left in me. Then there came again and touched me one like the appearance of a man, and he strengthened me, ... "*
> *-- Daniel 10:17-18*

I often experienced physical reactions when angels would come. It took a period of time for my physical body to get used to their presence. In the early angelic encounters, I would be left frozen, glued to the floor and too weak to move. On other occasions, my entire body vibrated as the angels ministered to me. In the months that followed, I gradually became more functional when the angels were with me.

Many times angels would pour oils on me or give me something to eat or drink in the spirit. These things seemed to strengthen my body when in the presence of God's glory and power.

> *"But thou, son of man, hear what I say unto thee; Be not thou rebellious like that rebellious house: open thy mouth, and eat that I give thee. And when I looked, behold, an hand was sent unto me; and, lo, a roll of a book was therein; And he spread it before me; and it was written within and without: and there was written therein lamentations, and mourning, and woe. Moreover he said unto me, Son of man, eat that thou findest; eat this roll, and go speak unto the house of Israel. So I opened my mouth, and he caused me to eat that roll."*
> *-- Ezekiel 2:8-3:2*

"And I went unto the angel, and said unto him, Give me the little book. And he said unto me, Take it, and eat it up; and it shall make thy belly bitter, but it shall be in thy mouth sweet as honey. And I took the little book out of the angel's hand, and ate it up; and it was in my mouth sweet as honey: and as soon as I had eaten it, my belly was bitter. And he said unto me, Thou must prophesy again before many peoples, and nations, and tongues, and kings."
-- Revelation 10:9-11

Today I feel the angels' presence, but rarely have physical manifestations when they are near. The Lord wants us to be able to stand and minister even though everyone else may fall to the floor as the weight of His glory comes into a service. Remember the priests in the temple in I Kings 8:11 who could not stand to minister because of God's glory? We must be able to function in these intense outpourings. God is getting our bodies ready now for what is just ahead for the church and the world.

The one constant about the angels is that they love to be involved in prayer. This should not be surprising considering that intercession is one of the main focuses of Jesus. He is continually interceding for us.

"...It is Christ that died, yea rather, that is risen again, who is even at the right hand of God, who also maketh intercession for us."
-- Romans 8:34

Remember in the Garden of Gethsemane the angels that came to minister to Jesus as He interceded. It does not seem to matter whether one prays alone or with a group, the angels love to get involved. Many times the angels have joined me while I am still in my car or climbing the stairs to my favorite prayer spot in our balcony, ready to take me places in the spirit or do whatever the Lord purposed for my prayer time that day.

On several occasions the angels told us their names. This is a regular occurrence with our pastor and happens with me less often, even many of our intercessors have received the names of the angels who have ministered with them. Although this is not that important, I think it is God's way of telling us that we are to have a more familiar relationship with the angels. God is removing the mystery of who these beings really are and drawing us into His kingdom.

Let me be quick to say that we DO NOT pray to angels. It is the Lord who sends the angels. They are assigned of the Lord. You cannot command a specific angel to come. Sometimes God has sent the same angel to me again and again, and at other times He has sent a new angel. There have been times when God had us initiate conversations with the angels. It is not something you look to do, the Lord prompts you to do it and you simply obey. There will be many times in the future when the Lord will send His angels to a service with a specific assignment to complete. God will instruct us what to say to them or we will simply say, "Do whatever the Lord has sent you to do." However, I believe our interaction and cooperation with the angels will become more involved.

One possible scenario is for an angel to bring a gift to the service, give it to the minister in charge and instruct the minister to give it to the intended recipient. Another scenario might be one in which the minister in charge would release the angel to bestow the gift directly. This type of partnership is what God intended for us to have with His angels.

In the early days, I was very concerned about the Lord thinking I was seeking experiences with the angels over communing with Him. However, the more I sought Him the more encounters I would have with the angels. The Lord kept telling me these encounters were all of Him and I need not worry. If the Lord is the One in control, we do not need to be anxious about encounters with angels. The Lord is commissioning His children to minister with them. This is His purpose, not ours. The Lord will see to it that this ministry begins functioning throughout the body of Christ. The question is, "Who will cooperate and take the necessary risks and criticism for stepping into it? Will you?"

As the angels make their presence more obvious, there is a natural tendency to ask them questions. The Heavenly Father does not have a problem with this. Some of our intercessors have asked the angels questions and received answers. An angel told a lady in our church that she could ask questions as long as they pertained to her life and purpose. I personally do not ask questions unless I am prompted to do so by the Holy Spirit. The book of Zechariah clearly demonstrates this truth[1]. Zechariah asked many questions of the angels sent to reveal God's plan to him. The angels answered all his questions.

The Lord is guarding over this ministry. I know that some could easily go off the deep end and get "way out there," out of God's will and God's way; however, I believe that if a person is submitted to the Lord and to the leadership in their church, they will be safe.

The Lord has encouraged me all along the way to step out in faith. He has never scolded or chastened me in the area of learning to minister with His angels. This is not a pure science, and there are no manuals that I know of on how to do this "properly." One certainly cannot find a course on "ministering with angels" in Bible schools or seminaries. This is new terrain for the church of the twenty-first century. We know ministering with angels is not "new under the sun" but is rapidly becoming more prevalent across the body of Christ.

As the angels have come into our prayer times and services, they have brought many things from the Lord. They often pour anointings on people. Sometimes they bring a gift that has the name of the recipient written on it. Other times, angels have brought crowns, ointments that they rub on your head; they also put things in and on your spirit. I have been given a tablet and told to write things on it. On other occasions, I have been given things to drink and even scrolls to eat. Once I received many swords to be given to the saints and once a mantle that I was told to put on our pastor.

This is quite exciting. Pastor Crawford often receives gifts from the angels for various people in the congregation. In many ways this operates like a word of knowledge.

The angelic activity and ministry we are seeing now more closely aligns with biblical accounts of angelic activity than does the current fad of angelic rescues. For example, Jesus says the angels are reapers of the end time harvest.

> *"The enemy that sowed them is the devil; the harvest is the*
> *end of the world; and the reapers are the angels."*
> *-- Matthew 13:39*

When angels come into our prayer times, they electrify the atmosphere and moves the intercession up to higher levels of intensity. When the angels are around, you pray more powerfully but with less effort on your part. When they arrive to assist in our prayers, often the languages we are speaking suddenly change to the angels' language. In a moment's time, if there are several angels around, there could be a dozen or more different languages (divers tongues) come forth out of one intercessor's mouth.

> *"Though I speak with the tongues of men and of angels..."*
> *-- 1 Corinthians 13:1*

Having angels around has become a regular occurrence in our church. Their involvement in our prayers and intercession is a fact. In the early days, the knowledge that angels were present was often not discerned or recognized. People would recognize and speak about the incredible heightened moments of intercession, but in the very beginning God did not reveal that this was a direct result of angels being present.

AUTHORITY STRUCTURE

The Lord always works through the authority structure. God is very big on establishing and flowing through authority. First, the Lord revealed the angels to our Pastor and later to me, as the Associate Pastor. It was many months later before the intercessors and congregation began discerning the presence of the angels themselves.

I do not want you to miss this point. This is KEY! Angels only follow the God-ordained authority structure. God's angels will not go to anyone who is or will try to usurp authority. A word of warning: Satan's angels -- disguised as angels of light – WILL!

While the angels first made their presence known in our prayer meetings, they eventually began showing up in our services, too. Up to this point they might have been seen or perceived, but as yet they were not interacting in ministry. However, it was not long before they began ministering with us in the services.

For instance, during a Wednesday night service seven angels came and stood in a group to the left of our pastor as he spoke. Pastor saw them, paused and waited to see why the angels had come but they made no indication they were going to do anything. So, he continued to preach his message. Toward the end of the message, the Holy Spirit told me that the seven angels had been sent to minister with me and would be released to minister when I went up front.

Knowing the Lord only works through the line of authority, I prayed. I did not rush up and interrupt the service; in fact, I made no indication to anyone that the Lord had just spoken to me. Instead, I told the Lord if this was truly of Him, Pastor would call me to the front and I would gladly do His bidding. In the process of dismissing the congregation, Pastor looked over and asked me if I had anything from the Lord to share tonight? I went up front and asked those that were called to the ministry to come forward. The presence of the Lord poured into the sanctuary. After the service, Pastor told me that as I came to the front the angels moved from their fixed positions, flanked me and began pouring anointings on the people, as well as on me.

On another occasion, during a Saturday evening prayer time, a group of demons came into the sanctuary. (Unfortunately, we have learned that demons are more faithful to come to prayer meetings than a lot of Christians.) Before these demons had a chance to do anything, a host of God's angels came flying down and fought with them and within a few seconds all the demons were gone. There was not a specific prayer prayed to cause this to happen. God was doing what He does so wonderfully, caring for us and protecting us.[2]

In this book the Lord is having me share an introductory level of interacting with His angels. I will be sharing briefly about how the angels will be ministering with us in healings and signs and wonders. I will also be sharing about the angels' assistance in spiritual warfare. God wants His children to become comfortable relating with the angels on a day-to-day basis. This will soon become a regular part of our life so we must be ready and trained for it.

From what the Lord has been revealing, we have not even started to realize what God has prepared for us. The Lord is opening up His heavens right now for His children to step in and partake of His kingdom. There will be many naysayers, but that does not negate the open invitation from the Lord.

For the first few years after the initial Brownsville trip, Pastor Crawford and I were the only ones in our church to receive extensive training from the angels. Our congregation was being tested, sifted and gifted to be people of worship and intercession. The call to be in an army and not in a nursery school was answered by many.

> *"For when for the time ye ought to be teachers, ye have need that one teach you again which be the first principles of the oracles of God; and are become such as have need of milk, and not of strong meat."*
>
> *-- Hebrews 5:12*

Pastor Crawford's training and experiences with the angelic differed from mine in several ways. First, Pastor Crawford is a seer. He sees into the spirit realm in ways that are off the spiritual eye chart. He sees angels, the Heavenly Father, Jesus, the elders, and many structures in the spirit realm. His ability to see has enabled him to be incredibly accurate in words of knowledge and in the prophetic. Second, even though he has been put through some grueling warfare, his training has come from the perspective of the throne of God and how to visibly see God's kingdom come to earth. His calling is one of establishing God's kingdom on the earth.

When I say "establishing God's kingdom on the earth," I am referring directly to Jesus' prayer of "Thy kingdom come." We very much believe both the books of Daniel and Revelation in which a literal tribulation, a literal antichrist and an actual battle at Armageddon is prophesied.

My training, on the other hand, has almost exclusively been in spiritual warfare. Many times I have been in one-on-one combat with demons. The warfare God has been teaching me is different from what is normally taught or even practiced in the body of Christ. My calling is one of training God's army of saints.

God has graciously given us both revelatory and cutting edge assignments in the heavenlies. There are times that what we do overlaps one another as we pursue what God has given us to do individually. However, most of the time God has us focused on our own jobs. I fully submit myself to my pastor's leadership. This is not a negotiable area with God. The enemy has desperately tried to get me to pull away from my pastor, but through the grace of God, the Lord has kept us close. Our relationship has been described as a double-edged sword.

"Iron sharpeneth iron; so a man sharpeneth the countenance of his friend."

-- Proverbs 27:17

Be assured, dear friend, you must stay in line with your spiritual authority. One of the best books I have read on this subject is <u>A Tale of Three Kings</u> by Gene Edwards.[3] I highly recommend it.

---

[1] Zechariah's questions to angels: Zechariah 1:9, 19, 21, 2:2, 4:11, 5:6, 6:4,
[2] **John G. Lake, His Life, His Sermons, His Boldness of Faith**, Kenneth Copeland Publications, Fort Worth, Texas, 1994. (p. 140)
[3] **A Tale of Three Kings**, by Gene Edwards, Christian Books, Augusta, Maine, 1980.

Chapter 6

MINISTERING WITH ANGELS

"And he said unto me, These sayings are *faithful and true: and the Lord God of the holy prophets sent his angel to shew unto his servants the things which must shortly be done."*
-- Revelation 22:6

One of God's stated purposes and callings for our church has been to birth the revelation of the ministry of the believers with angels. God has been preparing us for over four years for this assignment. God is teaching us about the angels in a variety of ways. Those with previous experiences and saints who have never interacted with angels are either sensing or perceiving their presence.

As we have been baptized into this ministry, the Lord has shown us some powerful things. First of all, the Holy Spirit is the administrator and empowering agent of the angelic realm. What I mean is, nothing happens in the angelic realm without His oversight and permission. You cannot receive a visit from one of the Lord's angels without it being totally sanctioned and initiated by God. Will an angel of the Lord ever tell you something that is not a message from God? No! One of the main functions of angels is to deliver messages directly from God; they are not paraphrased or revised by the angel in any form. Can we trust one of the Lord's angels implicitly? YES!

Some may say, "Well, God just does not do things that way. He has never sent an angel to me, so why should I believe you?" Others might think, "The only angel I have encountered helped me in a serious situation. I just do not believe angels do all these other things you mentioned." If that line of reasoning were sound, then why do you believe the Bible? The scriptures themselves declare that the prophets believed many things they had never seen and often did not understand the revelations they were given from God. Even angels do not understand all the mysteries of God and desire to look into them.

> *"Of which salvation the prophets have enquired and searched diligently, who prophesied of the grace that should come unto you: Searching what, or what manner of time the Spirit of Christ which was in them did signify, when it testified beforehand the sufferings of Christ, and the glory that should follow. Unto whom it was revealed, that not unto themselves, but unto us they did minister the things, which are now reported unto you by them that have preached the gospel unto you with the Holy Ghost sent down from heaven; which things the angels desire to look into."*
> -- *1 Peter 1:10-12*

God asks us an entirely different question. It is the question He asked Job,

> *"Where wast thou when I laid the foundations of the earth? declare, if thou hast understanding."*
> - *Job 38:4*

I encourage you to read the rest of that chapter. Basically God says to Job, you have no idea what I do or how I do it, so who are you to question Me? My friend, you cannot judge the validity of God's work by your own experiences or knowledge. You must judge based on scripture. How well does a teaching or ministry line up with the truths in God's Word? Not just the scriptures you have underlined and have heard preached over and over again, but the whole Word of God. Jesus told us that the works that He did we would do also. Jesus ministered with angels and God wants the church to minister with angels as well.

"Verily, verily, I say unto you, He that believeth on me, the works that I do shall he do also; and greater works than these shall he do; because I go unto my Father."
-- John 14:12

It has been amazing how God has shown up on our behalf. I have not had to convince anyone in our church that angels exist and are ministering to the saints. The angels are very obvious and overt. God is reestablishing this ministry throughout the Church, whether believers accept it and walk in it or not.

In 1 Corinthians Paul speaks of the "gifts of the Holy Spirit." The Spirit is said to give these gifts, "severally, as He will." My understanding has been that these gifts were given directly to the believer without any "middle man" so to speak. However, this assumption may not be entirely correct. Throughout the Bible there are many stories and parables in which servants are employed to distribute gifts or fulfill the desires and commandments of a father. Examples such as Abraham sending his servant to find a wife for Isaac (Genesis 24), Jesus' parables of the wedding supper, and the great banquet (Matthew 22, Luke 14) all depict servants being sent to do their master's bidding. This is the primary work of the angels...doing God's bidding. The angels are helping us understand this dynamic of the working of the Holy Spirit.

We must look again at the administrative functions of the Holy Spirit. He gives gifts severally as He wills. The Holy Spirit sends angels to deliver gifts of healing, miracles, signs and wonders, anointings, and even prophetic words or messages. This is only a small sampling of what the angels are given to do. I am not suggesting that angels are one and the same as the Holy Spirit; that would be ludicrous. The angels merely function as His agents. They are truly sent to *"...minister for them who shall be heirs of salvation"* (Hebrews 1:14).

Jesus said He went about doing what He saw His Father doing. Could it be that part of this was watching the angels to see what they were bringing to people? What God has been teaching us is that many times the angels, ministering under the direction and power of the Holy Spirit, are the ones who deliver healing to someone. If you think about this for a moment, you will see that this wonderful safeguard would keep us from becoming prideful in our healing ministries. When we see and realize that we are just partnering with the Lord's angels and a healing that God sends for someone has nothing to do with us, we should be humbled. We will be able to stand back and describe to the congregation how the angels are going about the auditorium bringing anointings for healing. We are not really doing anything anyway, except being obedient.

Unlike men who will believe someone who claims to be speaking for God, but is not, angels know God and know when God the Holy Spirit is speaking to them through a human vessel. They will not accept instructions that come from the spirit of a man, only instructions that come from the Spirit of God.

DO NOT misunderstand what is being said. God wants us to minister with His angels to fulfill His purposes. However, there are requirements. I must be submitted to my God-given authority. My mind must be renewed. My emotions need to be submitted to the Lord. My flesh must die and I must be walking in the Lord's ways and not my own.

PROGRESSIVE REVELATION

There is no doubt we are living in the final days. There is going to be more revelation of God's kingdom, the spirit realm and the Word of God than this world could ever imagine. There is nothing that will be added to the Word, but there will be countless passages where God's deeper meaning will be revealed to His children. Throughout time God has been building a clearer and more elaborate revelation of Himself. Adam and Eve were given a glimpse; to Abraham more was revealed, to Moses even more. Throughout the time of the judges, the kings, and the captivity, more and more revelation came. When Jesus walked on the earth, a tremendous new revelation came regarding God's plan of salvation. On the day of Pentecost a whole new dimension of the Holy Spirit was revealed. Years later the revelation came of the Gentiles being included in the plan of salvation. Many years later the revelation came to John of what would happen in the last days.

"And I heard, but I understood not: then said I, O my Lord, what shall be the end of these things? And he said, Go thy way, Daniel: for the words are closed up and sealed till the time of the end."
                                        -- Daniel 12:8-9

"That the God of our Lord Jesus Christ, the Father of glory, may give unto you the spirit of wisdom and revelation in the knowledge of him: The eyes of your understanding being enlightened; that ye may know what is the hope of his calling, and what the riches of the glory of his inheritance in the saints,..."
                                        -- Ephesians 1:17-18

Scripture teaches that God reveals things line upon line, precept upon precept. We also know that God is not finished revealing things to His church.

"But as it is written, Eye hath not seen, nor ear heard, neither have entered into the heart of man, the things which God hath prepared for them that love him."
                                        -- 1 Corinthians 2:9

"For precept must be upon precept, precept upon precept; line upon line, line upon line; here a little, and there a little: ..."
                                        -- Isaiah 28:10

There is a greater depth of knowing that is coming to the Church. The angels will be coming to unveil many secrets that have been sealed up and to reveal specifically what is going to happen in these last days. This is not a new thing. Five times in Revelation alone an angel was sent to John to show him things that would happen. The very first verse of Revelation says an angel brought the revelation.

"The Revelation of Jesus Christ, which God gave unto him, to shew unto his servants things which must shortly come to pass; and he sent and <u>signified it by his angel</u> unto his servant   John: ..."
-- *Revelation 1:1*

Then in chapter 4 John says,

"After this I looked, and, behold, a door was opened in heaven: and the first voice which I heard was as it were of a trumpet talking with me; which said, Come up hither, and I will shew thee things which must be hereafter."
-- *Revelation 4:1*

Again in chapter 17 John reports an angel revealing revelation to him.

"And there came <u>one of the seven angels</u> which had the seven vials, and <u>talked with me</u>, saying unto me, Come hither; I will shew unto thee the judgment of the great whore that sitteth upon many waters: ..."
-- *Revelation 17:1*

Another of the seven angels with the seven vials came to John in chapter 21.

"And there came unto me <u>one of the seven angels</u> which had the seven vials full of the seven last plagues, and talked with me, saying, Come hither, I will shew thee the bride, the Lamb's wife."
-- *Revelation 21:9*

Finally, Revelation 22:6 records that God sent His angel to show unto His servants the things that shortly must be.

> *"And he said unto me, These sayings* are *faithful and true: and the Lord God of the holy prophets <u>sent his angel to shew unto his servants the things which must shortly be done.</u>"*
> *-- Revelation 22:6*

Notice, the final passage does not say the "sending" was done <u>to John,</u> but <u>to His servants.</u> Just like in Revelation, specific instructions and details will be given to God's servants about the forthcoming judgments on the world. The Church will be called on to intercede for all these things.

Angels, unlike man, always obey God. They obey to the finest detail. If they are present in a church service, then we know that God sent them. There is coming a time when it will be common place for God to use His servants, the saints, jointly with angels in ministry. Remember when the seven angels came to minister in our service that night? It was my obedience to the Holy Spirit that released the angels to do what they had been sent to do. If I had not obeyed God, the angels would not have accomplished what they came to do that night. I would have been disobedient and would have quenched the Holy Spirit. In like manner, saints will be used of God to cooperate with the angels in ministry. The point is not that angels will be obeying us, because they will not obey the spirit of man.

> *"For what man knoweth the things of a man, save the spirit of man which is in him? even so the things of God knoweth no man, but the Spirit of God. Now we have received, not the spirit of the world, but the spirit which is of God; that we might know the things that are freely given to us of God."*
> *-- 1 Corinthians 2:11-12*

54

"If any man speak, let him speak as the oracles of God; if any man minister, let him do it as of the ability which God giveth: that God in all things may be glorified through Jesus Christ, to whom be praise and dominion for ever and ever. Amen."

-- 1 Peter 4:11

Angels obey the voice of the Spirit of God that is within us. This interaction will become a regular occurrence for believers that enter into this higher level of ministry with the Lord's angels.

For example, in the scriptures God instructed Ezekiel to command the wind, and then God tells us in Revelation that there are angels who hold the winds.

"Then said he unto me, Prophesy unto the wind, prophesy, son of man, and say to the wind, Thus saith the Lord GOD; Come from the four winds, O breath, and breathe upon these slain, that they may live."

-- Ezekiel 37:9

"And after these things I saw four angels standing on the four corners of the earth, holding the four winds of the earth, that the wind should not blow on the earth, nor on the sea, nor on any tree."

-- Revelation 7:1

Why would God have men tell angels to do something? Why not just tell them Himself? These are good questions. I personally believe God had already told the angels Himself. That is how the angels know whether the person they are ministering with is truly listening to and speaking God's words or not. Then why does God want a person to tell the angel to do something? In Genesis, to whom did God give dominion over the earth?

> *"And God blessed them, and God said unto them, Be fruitful, and multiply, and replenish the earth, and subdue it: and have dominion over the fish of the sea, and over the fowl of the air, and over every living thing that moveth upon the earth."*
>
> *-- Genesis 1:28*

God gave dominion over the earth to man. We also believe the doctrine of "free will" which simply states God will not violate man's will. For example, man must ask to be saved. This principle is also true on a corporate level. God will not violate man's dominion of the earth. God must have someone agree with Him and ask Him to move in situations on the earth. We cannot force our will on God and God will not force His will on us. Instead, God finds a yielded vessel willing to declare His will into a situation. Once God's will and word go forth from a human vessel, God can release angels to accomplish that word. In the case of illness, we know it is God's will to bring healing. At times He could instruct us to release the angels sent to minister healing to those in the service.

Let me assure you, someone cannot just get up and begin releasing angels to minister. If the Lord God has not instructed that person to release the angels, the angels simply will not go. Angels only obey God.

> *"Bless the Lord, ye his angels, that excel in strength, <u>that do his commandments, hearkening unto the voice of his word</u>. Bless ye the Lord, all ye his hosts; ye ministers of his, that do his pleasure."*
>
> *-- Psalm 103:20-21*

"Who is gone into heaven, and is on the right hand of God; angels and authorities and powers being made subject unto him."

-- 1 Peter 3:22

It is difficult for us to understand that God sometimes speaks to us through the angelic. You might ask, "Isn't that what the Father, Jesus and the Holy Spirit are supposed to do?" We must be careful not to think that God is being aloof when He chooses to use angels to speak to us instead of speaking to us directly. Why does God need a middleman? We must understand that angels were created to serve God and as scripture reveals were assigned to *"...minister for them who shall be heirs of salvation"* (Hebrews 1:14). The Lord loves to see His angels minister with men. The fact of the matter is when an angel speaks to us, it is God Almighty speaking. If it were not for the revelation and discernment God is giving, we would never know the difference. Angels are God's messengers. We find this truth depicted over and over again in scripture. Gabriel, for instance, brought Daniel messages.

"And I heard a man's voice between the banks of Ulai, which called, and said, Gabriel, make this man to understand the vision."

-- Daniel 8:16

"Yea, whiles I was speaking in prayer, even the man Gabriel, whom I had seen in the vision at the beginning, being caused to fly swiftly, touched me about the time of the evening oblation. And he informed me, and talked with me, and said, O Daniel, I am now come forth to give thee skill and understanding."

-- Daniel 9:21-22

Gabriel was also sent to Zacharias and Joseph with messages.

> *"And the angel answering said unto him, I am Gabriel, that stand in the presence of God; and am sent to speak unto thee, and to shew thee these glad tidings."*
>
> -- *Luke 1:19*

> *"And in the sixth month the angel Gabriel was sent from God unto a city of Galilee, named Nazareth, To a virgin espoused to a man whose name was Joseph, of the house of David; and the virgin's name was Mary."*
>
> -- *Luke 1:26-27*

These are only a few of the many, many times angels were sent to bring messages to people.

Angels for the most part work in anonymity, with the exceptions of Michael and Gabriel. These are the two angels the Bible mentions by name. Why? Typically angels function as God's messengers with the priority being the message and not the messenger. It is only because it is the sovereign will of God in these last days that we are seeing the unveiling of this incredible heavenly host. As the Lord reveals these angels, many of them will be allowed to tell us their names. For many saints these angels will become very close.

Although angels are not all-knowing like God, they do have supernatural knowing ability. For one thing, they can know your thoughts. Often angels will speak to you spirit to spirit. In Luke 1:29-30 it says, *"And when she saw him, she was troubled at his saying, and cast in her mind what manner of salutation this should be. And the angel said unto her, Fear not, Mary: for thou hast found favour with God."* At times God will allow your mind to understand what the angels are saying. There will also be times when you have a question in your heart, and the angel will answer it without you speaking out loud. **The best way to look at this is that the Holy Spirit is omniscient and He simply tells the angels what you are thinking.**

Angels are not omniscient or omnipresent but need directions and instructions from God. We observe from scripture that all three members of the Godhead give angels instructions. Specifically, God the Holy Spirit dwells in born again, spirit-filled believers, and has chosen to speak through these purified, dedicated, yielded human vessels. Remember I Peter 4:11 says, *"If any man speak, let him speak as the oracles of God..."*

Over time I have learned that angels know whether or not you can see in the spirit realm. If they know you cannot see them, they use other methods to get your attention. This happens when an angel is near you and you perceive or discern the angel but do not see him. You must listen very carefully to see if he is saying or doing something or needs you to say or do something. The angels exercise great patience as we learn to interact with them. **Here again, I want to emphasize that we do not have to see angels in order to minister with them.**

Numerous times during prayer various angels have come to give me weapons, gifts or anointings. Quite often, when I step out in faith and receive them, I sense things in my spirit. It could be the warmth of the angel's anointing, the jolt of his presence or a sudden explosion of joy. One of the elemental understandings we must have in order to minister with angels is that it requires our faith. Without faith it is impossible to gain access into this realm.

59

An angel of God does not come to a person unless God sends them. However, we must always be on guard to discern an angel of light or other demon masquerading as an angel of the Lord. Believe me, Satan's dark angels intend to fool you and lead you astray. Paul referred to these dark angels who came from Satan's throne in the second heaven when he said:

> *"Which is not another; but there be some that trouble you, and would pervert the gospel of Christ. But though we, or an angel from heaven, preach any other gospel unto you than that which we have preached unto you, let him be accursed."*
> *-- Galatians 1:7-8*

What God has given His church is a powerful gift of discerning of spirits. We have also been given the test that is in the Word.

> *"Hereby know ye the Spirit of God: Every spirit that confesseth that Jesus Christ is come in the flesh is of God: ..."*
> *-- 1 John 4:2*

> *"Wherefore I give you to understand, that no man speaking by the Spirit of God calleth Jesus accursed: and that no man can say that Jesus is the Lord, but by the Holy Ghost. "*
> *-- 1 Corinthians 12:3*

Just like moving in the prophetic and other giftings of the Holy Spirit, we must exercise the discernment gift in order to become proficient in it. I remember one specific encounter involving a battle in which many demons were taken captive by the angels; afterwards I could still sense a powerful presence in the area. When I asked an angel beside me what I was sensing he said it was the ruling dark angel. He also instructed me to be careful because the dark angel could be very deceptive. **When this** demon got close to me, his presence registered "big time" in my spirit. To my amazement I felt a good presence, not an overpowering evil presence. Unlike other demons I've encountered, the languages he used in speaking to me sounded much like one of God's angels. I could barely detect the evil; however, God gave me the discernment to know this was an evil entity.

Angels bring messages from God. So whatever God's angel tells you is exactly what God wants you to hear. It is vital then that we learn how to listen to these messengers. To do this takes practice.

Often the distinction between God's actions and the angel's actions blur to the point where they seem synonymous. They appear synonymous because angels so exactly carry out God's instructions that they are actually a tool or agent. Angels do nothing of their own will or way, only God's will and way. This facet of angelic behavior is revealed in Exodus where Moses sees the burning bush. Note how verse two clearly states that it is an angel who is appearing to Moses, and the rest of the passage states over and over again that God called to Moses, God spoke to Moses.

> *"And the angel of the LORD appeared unto him in a flame of fire out of the midst of a bush: and he looked, and, behold, the bush burned with fire, and the bush was not consumed. And Moses said, I will now turn aside, and see this great sight, why the bush is not burnt. And when the LORD saw that he turned aside to see, God called unto him out of the midst of the bush, and said, Moses, Moses. And he said, Here am I."*
>
> *-- Exodus 3:2-4*

Ministering with Angels

Bear in mind, when humans interact in the spirit realm, they have difficulty being able to discern. Even the Apostle John got confused and often mistook a saint for an angel and vice-versa.

> *"And I fell at his feet to worship him. And he said unto me, See thou do it not: I am thy fellowservant, and of thy brethren that have the testimony of Jesus: worship God: for the testimony of Jesus is the spirit of prophecy."*
> *-- Revelation 19:10*

> *"Then saith he unto me, See thou do it not: for I am thy fellowservant, and of thy brethren the prophets, and of them which keep the sayings of this book: worship God."*
> *-- Revelation 22:9*

The point is not who is doing the ministry -- God Himself or God via one of His agents -- an angel, patriarch, saint or believer. The point is God's purpose is being accomplished. The Bible teaches us that we are to pray for God's will to be done. It is prayer for God's will that obtains the ministry of angels.

> *"Thinkest thou that I cannot now pray to my Father, and he shall presently give me more than twelve legions of angels? But how then shall the scriptures be fulfilled, that thus it must be?"*
> *-- Matthew 26:53-54*

*"Peter therefore was kept in prison: <u>but prayer was made
without ceasing of the church unto God for him.</u> And when
Herod would have brought him forth, the same night Peter
was sleeping between two soldiers, bound with two chains:
and the keepers before the door kept the prison. And,
behold, the angel of the Lord came upon him, and a light
shined in the prison: and he smote Peter on the side, and
raised him up, saying, Arise up quickly. And his chains fell
off from his hands."*

-- Acts 12:5-7

When somebody first reads about God's people interacting with angels,
it will probably set off alarms. How can God use humans to release
angels into a situation? We must remember that we are the temple of the
Holy Spirit. The Holy Spirit can speak through us to the angels. We
should not look at this as giving orders, but as simply cooperating with
the Godhead and with His angels. It is a humbling thing to imagine that
God would use us to minister with His angels. God is training His
children for their eternal role to rule and reign with Him. I am not
saying we are ruling now, but God is preparing us for that day.

*"And hast made us unto our God kings and priests: and we
shall reign on the earth."*

-- Revelation 5:10

Did you know the Word says one day we will judge His angels?

*"Do ye not know that the saints shall judge the world? and if
the world shall be judged by you, are ye unworthy to judge
the smallest matters? Know ye not that we shall judge
angels? how much more things that pertain to this life?"*

-- 1 Corinthians 6:2-3

63

Ministering with Angels

There are many reasons why God is revealing His angels in this hour. For one thing we need their help. We cannot quote scripture at the devil and his forces and expect them to go running with their tails between their legs. The devil is not afraid of scripture. He is afraid of authority! The devil is quite articulate when it comes to knowing the Word of God. Satan even quoted scriptures to Jesus, the Word Incarnate, during His temptation in the wilderness. Unfortunately, Satan twists scripture. You can speak the Word of God to the devil but if he does not know you, you have a serious problem.

Acts 19 tells of the seven sons of Sceva who tried simply doing what Jesus did, and got themselves into big trouble.

> *"And the evil spirit answered and said, Jesus I know, and Paul I know; but who are ye? And the man in whom the evil spirit was leaped on them, and overcame them, and prevailed against them, so that they fled out of that house naked and wounded."*
>
> *-- Acts 19:15-16*

The evil spirit said to them, "Who are you?" The evil spirit knew who had authority and who did not. He knew who had already overcome the demonic in spiritual warfare and intercession and who had not. How does Satan know you are in authority and need to be reckoned with? Let me first remind you that earlier in this chapter I said the angels are sent to give you weapons, anointings and gifts. These can be seen in the spirit realm. Satan recognizes and fears the colorings that your spirit radiates. He observes the honors that the Lord has placed upon you and sees the specially crafted weapons that Jesus has given you. He eyes the markings on your spiritual vesture where the name of the Lord has been inscribed. He can tell that you have been with Jesus by the light that shines within you. Or, maybe it is the company of angels that follow you because you have gained authority and the Lord protects His prophets.

> *"Saying, Touch not mine anointed, and do my prophets no harm."*
> *-- Psalm 105:15*

> *"And Elisha prayed, and said, LORD, I pray thee, open his eyes, that he may see. And the LORD opened the eyes of the young man; and he saw: and, behold, the mountain was full of horses and chariots of fire round about Elisha."*
> *-- 2 Kings 6:17*

> *"For he shall give his angels charge over thee, to keep thee in all thy ways."*
> *-- Psalm 91:11*

Could it be that the devil has heard about your victories over some of his ardent warriors, warriors who have come back to him with wounds inflicted by some weapon unknown in the dark realm. Yes, the Lord is drawing His saints into the angelic battle of the ages. What do you mean? Hasn't that war already taken place? It may be time to re-evaluate our eschatology and open up our hearts to what God is revealing in these last days.

Let's review. If a holy angel comes to us, we know it has to be God's will and whatever he says has to be what God instructed him to say. Angels never act independently of the Lord. There are no exceptions! Ministering with God's angels is the safest ministry in which we could be involved. The hardest part of ministering with angels is learning how to recognize their presence. Even if you are not able to see the angels, the Lord can teach you how to interact with them. When an angel is sent to you, relax and enjoy the presence of the Lord that they emanate. Be expectant of what God may have sent them to tell you or to give you. Once you master this, you are on your way to discovering some incredible things in the kingdom of God.

Chapter 7

SUBMITTING TO AUTHORITY

"Thine, O LORD, is the greatness, and the power, and the glory, and the victory, and the majesty: for all that is in the heaven and in the earth is thine; thine is the kingdom, O LORD, and thou art exalted as head above all."
-- 1 Chronicles 29:11

In the early angelic encounters, when the angels had a message or delivery they would first go to Pastor Crawford for permission to approach me. Eventually the Lord told Pastor to authorize the angels to have free access to me without checking in with him first. This protocol is very crucial if you want the influx of the angelic in your church and your personal life. If the proper authority structure in your church is not in place, or if the leadership is not willing for angelic ministry involvement, there will be limited or no angelic ministry.

The angels are part of the most perfect order of authority. God established authority and angels fully comply and operate within this structure.

> *"And said, O LORD God of our fathers, art not thou God in heaven? and rulest not thou over all the kingdoms of the heathen? and in thine hand is there not power and might, so that none is able to withstand thee?"*
> *-- 2 Chronicles 20:6*

God has established authority structures throughout all of creation, on the earth, in heaven and in hell.

> *"And Jesus came and spake unto them, saying, All power is given unto me in heaven and in earth."*
> *-- Matthew 28:18*

Both the kingdom of heaven and the kingdom of darkness operate in levels of authority. Both angels and demons have rank. Angels are very respectful of all levels of God- established authority.

Angels will not go around the authority of the senior pastor to work with an associate pastor, board member, elder or member. They operate completely within the authority structure that God has established, flowing from the senior leader throughout the leadership and then into the congregation. It is imperative that congregational members DO NOT step out from under the established authorities.

> *"And Jesus saith unto him, I will come and heal him. The centurion answered and said, Lord, I am not worthy that thou shouldest come under my roof: but speak the word only, and my servant shall be healed. For I am a man under authority, having soldiers under me: and I say to this man, Go, and he goeth; and to another, Come, and he cometh; and to my servant, Do this, and he doeth it."*
> *-- Matthew 8:7-9*

I interact with many angels but I always remain in complete submission to my pastor. If I decided to rebel and start doing things on my own, I would lose my opportunity and ability to minister with the angels. God will not tolerate rebellion! If we want to walk in this angelic realm, we must be submitted to authority. I have witnessed some people that rebelled and they began having visitations and conversations with evil spirits. Unfortunately, the rebellious person did not discern that it was not an angel of the Lord until it was too late and the destruction of their life had begun.

The strategy of the kingdom of darkness is to get people to step outside of their authority structure. Stepping out of or rebelling against the authority God has placed in your life gives Satan the right to deceive and destroy you.

> *"And Samuel said, Hath the LORD as great delight in burnt offerings and sacrifices, as in obeying the voice of the LORD? Behold, to obey is better than sacrifice, and to hearken than the fat of rams. For rebellion is as the sin of witchcraft, and stubbornness is as iniquity and idolatry. Because thou hast rejected the word of the LORD, he hath also rejected thee from being king."*
> *-- 1 Samuel 15:22-23*

Let me illustrate this for a pastor and church who are desiring God to allow His kingdom to come into their midst. As we stated earlier, the senior pastor must desire this or it will not happen. Once the pastor submits himself to God's purposes for his life and that of his church, he is then ready. The church staff must also be committed. If there is resistance from a staff member, God will move them out. God will not allow grievous words to be spoken about this aspect of His kingdom.

Ministering with Angels

The operation of the ministry of angels is a vital part of the working of the Holy Spirit. God is extremely sensitive to words spoken against it and weighs these words heavily.

Once the pastoral staff is in line, God can begin moving throughout the leadership structure and the congregation. Every church will have a level of resistance against this move, but God is greater. God has a way of softening the hearts or moving those in resistance out of the way. The leadership MUST NOT react in their flesh, but allow the Holy Spirit to do His work. There are those in our congregation that in the beginning, I never guessed would be men and women of faith and power. Today, these same ones flow mightily in the things of the Lord and especially in ministering with angels. In addition, leaders must not try to hold on to someone that the Lord is transitioning out of their congregation. There are some who have left our church that I thought would have been leaders among us.

I can almost guarantee to you dear pastor, that once you focus on moving into the deeper realms of the Spirit, many under your leadership will balk and complain. Many will leave your church, which could include board members, teachers and your largest contributors. Yes, this will be a painful process! Everything in the natural will tell you that you have made a wrong decision. However, one thing is certain, God will show up in your prayer times in a way that will leave no doubt He is pleased with this transformation of your church.

When you accept the invitation to enter into this dimension of God's kingdom, relationships will be tested. In cases where a believing husband wants to pursue God with a passion and the believing wife does not, they will be forced to make a decision to go or stay. Although there are exceptions, many times their decision will result in losing the couple. There must be agreement within a marriage. Why? Because the Lord wants unity in His body and absolutely does not want any level of rebellion. In cases where the believer has an unbelieving spouse, this is not as much of an issue.

> *"For the unbelieving husband is sanctified by the wife, and the unbelieving wife is sanctified by the husband: else were your children unclean; but now are they holy."*
> *-- 1 Corinthians 7:14*

A pastor may find that his dearest friends are on the other side of the issue. You must be willing to give up everything to go after God in this way. The Lord must be your only pursuit. This pursuit puts everything else aside. Good desires must give way to God's desires.

As we have said, the angels are extremely sensitive to flowing in the authority structure whether in a nuclear family unit or a more complex structure such as a church. The Lord's angels are even respectful of the authority structure of the kingdom of darkness. The angels of the Lord recognize the authority that dark angels carried before the fall. Angels do not rail at demons or indiscriminately strike out at any demon that happens to cross their path. Jude 1:9 best demonstrates this fact when it says, *"Yet Michael the archangel, when contending with the devil he disputed about the body of Moses, durst not bring against him a railing accusation, but said, The Lord rebuke thee."* Angels will wait until another angel from the Lord of equal or higher rank to their demonic counterpart comes to give the command about what to do with their enemy. In the Old Testament, the angel sent to bring an answer to Daniel was prevented from getting through because of the higher rank

71

and power of the demonic Prince of Persia. It was necessary that Michael the archangel come to his aid (Daniel 10:13-21).

The bottom line is that angels respect authority. Pastor, you have nothing to fear when the angels of God start pouring into your church. You will not have to worry about the upper hand being given to another leader who might circumvent your authority. The enemy has done his best to prevent this operation of the ministry of angels with man. He has perverted the truth and created all kinds of rebellion within churches, which has prevented angels from ministering like they could.

Pastor, you must first find out to whom you are submitted. Are you submitted first of all to God and to what God wants? Or are you submitted to your own vision, to the vision of your board or to the vision of a wealthy giver? You must be honest with yourself. Who are you really following? Is your church ultimately receiving its direction from an organization or God Himself? Once you make a decision to follow God's voice, it will mean major changes in your personal life and in your church.

You can be assured that the angels know whether you are obedient to the voice of the Lord or not. You cannot expect a visitation and the ultimate habitation of the kingdom of God without an unshakable commitment to the purposes of Almighty God.

God will eventually help each church to get its substructures (i.e., various ministries and programs) into His order. To do this, the Lord will reveal to the pastor the spiritual authority and anointings that He has given to each member. Once these giftings are identified, members will be transitioned into their proper positions within the church. A lot of problems and attacks that churches endure result from people being placed in positions of authority based on natural or worldly qualifications. These qualifications would include a person's education, age, and even how long they have been saved. The Lord has taught us that a person can be saved for 30 years and still be feeding from the spiritual bottle.

> *"And I, brethren, could not speak unto you as unto spiritual,*
> *but as unto carnal, even as unto babes in Christ. I have fed*
> *you with milk, and not with meat: for hitherto ye were not*
> *able to bear it, neither yet now are ye able."*
> *-- 1 Corinthians 3:1-2*

I can already hear alarms going off! "How can we place someone younger and with less experience into a position of authority in our church?" It is crucial that we see with spiritual eyes. We must place people where God purposed them to minister. There are going to be many young who come in and quickly soar to spiritual heights. They will begin eating meat and desiring the deeper things of God and will not be satisfied with anything less. Those that are sucking the bottle will become jealous and criticize the younger and more passionate members.

Pastor, this is where you will have to make a tough choice. Will you listen to those who have been your supporters through the many years but want to keep things the same? Or, will you listen to the Spirit of God and step out on faith, allowing God to gift these younger ones in the Lord and get the church moving in God's direction? **Do not misunderstand me. Age is not the qualifier. Spiritual maturity, obedience to God, submission to authority, intimacy and communion with God, these are the qualifiers. God looks on the heart!**

> *"But the LORD said unto Samuel, Look not on his countenance, or on the height of his stature; because I have refused him: for the LORD seeth not as man seeth; for man looketh on the outward appearance, but the LORD looketh on the heart."*   *-- 1 Samuel 16:7*

Here again we must ask ourselves if this is all worth it. Pastor, please ask yourself this question before you start making any changes. "Do I want to go through hell to have heaven come down?" You must have a personal commitment that basically says, "God, I would rather die than not commit to Your purposes." As a pastor you must be willing to lose staff and congregational members. God's will must come first. There are no exceptions.

Can you take the pressure of family members contending with you over your decision to go after God? Jesus warned that is exactly what is coming.

> *"For I am come to set a man at variance against his father, and the daughter against her mother, and the daughter in law against her mother in law. And a man's foes shall be they of his own household. He that loveth father or mother more than me is not worthy of me: and he that loveth son or daughter more than me is not worthy of me. And he that taketh not his cross, and followeth after me, is not worthy of me."*
>
> *-- Matthew 10:35-38*

This passage was spoken in the context of what serving God would be like in the last days. While we are to pray that our immediate family and extended families will stay unified, we must also be ready to keep on going even if it means going on alone.

Chapter 8

ENTERING THE SPIRIT REALM

"It is not expedient for me doubtless to glory. I will come to visions and revelations of the Lord. I knew a man in Christ above fourteen years ago, (whether in the body, I cannot tell; or whether out of the body, I cannot tell: God knoweth;) such an one caught up to the third heaven. And I knew such a man, (whether in the body, or out of the body, I cannot tell: God knoweth;)..."

-- 2 Corinthians 12:1-3

As time went along the angels began talking to me. Sometimes I would hear their voices in my spirit, while at other times they would interrupt me as I prayed in the Spirit. This became a daily occurrence.

What did they say? Usually it was words of encouragement and affirmation of His love for me. Sometimes it was more riveting. One day while I was praying at the church, two angels came and took me in the spirit to a place where a man was laying in the street, dying from either a gunshot or knife wound. After the Lord had me pray for him, I was taken back to the church.

As these visitations continued the level of interaction with the angels increased in both duration and intensity. I began to sense them more regularly as I walked about the church, praying. Many times their presence would knock me right to the floor! It was like walking into an electric field. Over time they started bringing gifts and anointings.

All along the way the Lord reassured me that these angelic visitations were of Him and that they would continue to occur. As the months went by, it was not uncommon for an angel to sit in a pew next to me and talk. However, most of the time they came when there was a particular mission or training exercise for me to complete.

During the first year in this new move of God, we experienced intense warfare during our times of intercession. Our prayers were loud and at times quite violent. It was not unusual for me to come out of these prayer times with my shirt soaked in sweat. This particular kind of praying was intense.

After many more months of training me in the spirit to be sensitive to the presence of angels, the Lord began taking me down into hell through spiritual openings called portals. There were times when I knew the angels of the Lord were with me and at other times I was not sure. I was taken to various places in hell where I saw hooded beings and various other demons and in one instance an assassin spirit sitting on his throne. When he noticed me coming, he got up and walked over to a portal opening, stepped into it and then vanished. I went down different corridors where lost souls were imprisoned. I was not asked to spend a great amount of time in hell. There was warfare, but a lot of my time was spent merely observing. I have to admit I was certainly relieved when the tours of hell were finally finished.

In between the missions on which I was sent, the angels came and taught me about spiritual warfare. They often brought weapons to be used while on these spiritual missions. There were many different kinds and sizes of swords brought to me. In addition, I was taught many hand and body movements -- similar to martial arts. I am sure I looked very strange in our church balcony during our times of intercession as the angels and I went through this particular type of training.

Day by day I was interacting in the spirit realm with greater fluidity. My faith increased daily as I, by faith, participated and trained with the angels. Very often I would have to reach out and take weapons from the angels and practice using them. Sometimes I was given poles that were to be used as weapons. The angels were very patient with my slow progress. You have to understand these angels are very intelligent. They even have to slow down their languages so we are able to understand them.

Following the time spent warring in the spirit and observing activities in hell, I was taken to what some might refer to as "the second heaven." The angels took me through various passageways, gates and doorways. At each entrance there was at least one demon that I had to fight in order to pass through. The degree of struggle and the type of fighting skills needed varied at each entryway. Even though angels accompanied me, I had to do the fighting alone. The angels that were with me would usually tell me what to expect at each gate. These gated areas felt incredibly evil, but not nearly as evil as the terror I felt when I went through hell.

At some of the entrances the demons would put up a fierce fight. I have been cussed at, threatened, hit, stabbed and strangled by demons. Did I feel any pain? Absolutely! I know there are some who might not believe that what I am saying could possibly be true, but the fighting was very real. For example, when a demon attempted to strangle me, my breath would be physically cut off until I was able to break loose. I could actually feel my windpipe constricting. How did I break loose? Through the power of Jesus' name. Speaking the name of Jesus is not always easy to do when you are being choked. There were many days when I came out of intercession in pain and totally exhausted.

These encounters generated some serious conversations with the Lord. "What about all those scriptures on how we overcome the devil? 'No weapon formed against me...'.'" I was not only inexperienced but I was ignorant. I was flat out getting beat up. Do not misunderstand me, we were winning the battles but for some reason there were a lot of wounds being inflicted in the process. The Lord knew what He was doing. With every battle and every victory, my faith was being increased as was my authority in the spirit realm. As the weeks went by I felt less and less pain from these demonic encounters. I was also learning of other scriptures where many heroes of faith fought, were hurt, and even killed.

"Who through faith subdued kingdoms, wrought righteousness, obtained promises, stopped the mouths of lions, Quenched the violence of fire, escaped the edge of the sword, out of weakness were made strong, waxed valiant in fight, turned to flight the armies of the aliens. Women received their dead raised to life again: and others were tortured, not accepting deliverance; that they might obtain a better resurrection: And others had trial of cruel mockings and scourgings, yea, moreover of bonds and imprisonment: They were stoned, they were sawn asunder, were tempted, were slain with the sword: they wandered about in sheepskins and goatskins; being destitute, afflicted, tormented; (Of whom the world was not worthy:) they wandered in deserts, and in mountains, and in dens and caves of the earth. And these all, having obtained a good report through faith, received not the promise: ..."
-- Hebrews 11:33-39

Today, the warfare I encounter has a completely different affect on me. While I do not usually experience as many physical attacks as I used to, the enemy tends to attack my emotions instead. You may ask, "Why did the attacks change?" It is all a part of God's training plan for me and only He knows the reason for the next phase. I just trust God, then follow and obey Him no matter what He asks me to do in battle.

One of the greatest benefits of having angels with you as you move into second heaven warfare is, as your authority increases the angelic involvement in the fighting increases. When my training first began, I had to talk to the demons one-on-one. Very often they would threaten to kill my loved ones and me. The involvement of the angels eventually increased to the point where they began talking to the demons directly. If I had anything to say to the demon, I would tell it to the angel and he would speak for me. Can you see how each encounter required that I listen to the Lord and obey? I could not simply fight each new battle or complete each new mission the same way I did the last one. I had to stay tuned in to what God was saying to me daily.

Let me explain a word I introduced earlier in this chapter that will soon become a part of the Christian vocabulary. The word is "portal." A portal is a passageway in the spirit realm. There are portal highways in the heavenlies, portals that go down into hell, and portals that connect to one another here on the surface of the earth. The portals that are on earth and in hell are different than those which run through the heavenlies. The angels fly through these portals at lightening speeds. If you will remember, I mentioned the assassin spirit down in hell that walked into a portal there. I have seen this same being in other places in the heavenlies. The enemy has been using these portals for millennia. Scripture is filled with references to these openings.

> *"After this I looked, and, behold, a **door** was opened in heaven: and the first voice which I heard was as it were of a trumpet talking with me; which said, Come up hither, and I will shew thee things which must be hereafter."*
> *-- Revelation 4:1*

> *"So ye in like manner, when ye shall see these things come to pass, know that it is nigh, even at the <u>doors</u>."*
> *-- Mark 13:29*

The word "door" in both of these scriptures comes from the Greek word "thura."

> *Thura: (thoo'-rah); Strong's Greek #2374 apparently a primary word [compare "door"]; <u>a</u> portal or entrance (the opening or the closure, literal or figurative) :- door, gate.*

Either godly angels or demons guard the majority of these portals. One must have specific authority to access these portals. The demons can move up and down out of hell and in and around the earth via these portals.[1]

As the Lord had me go on these missions and I saw or traveled through these portals, to my amazement I saw multitudes of dark angels access the portal highways in the heavenlies. Human spirits also have access to some of these portals. Individuals who are in partnership with demons get into these portals using a method known as astral projection. This is an incredibly dangerous activity! It can be deadly! Besides suffering the eternal consequences of partnering with demons, one can prematurely age or even die in the process.[2]

Before angels began regularly visiting us and training us in spiritual warfare, we had not focused on how many times the words, "gates," "doors," "highways" and similar phrases are used in scripture. I began to realize that a great many of the missions the Lord's angels took me on were directly related to obtaining access to or control over these portals.

One of the things the Lord has led us to do is clearout blocked or contested portals that extend from the second heaven into the third heaven. The Bible specifically speaks of three heavens.

> *"He that descended is the same also that ascended up far above all heavens, that he might fill all things."*
> *-- Ephesians 4:10*

Derek Prince has a quick-read book, Spiritual Warfare,[3] which gives an excellent portrayal of how the heavens are divided. In this book, it is pointed out that the word "all" always refers to at least three parts.

Prince goes on to say that we need to realize Satan's headquarters are not in hell, but in the heavenlies: "The headquarters of Satan's kingdom is located between the visible heaven and the heaven of God's dwelling."[4] The "visible heaven" is the first heaven and the "heaven of God's dwelling" is the third heaven.

> *"For we wrestle not against flesh and blood, but against principalities, against powers, against the rulers of the darkness of this world, against spiritual wickedness in high places."*
> *-- Ephesians 6:12*

These "high places" are what we will refer to as the second heaven. In this verse, we also see that Satan's kingdom has definite levels of authority. Believe me, the enemy knows exactly what he is doing. Jesus even alluded to the cohesiveness of Satan's kingdom.

> *"And Jesus knew their thoughts, and said unto them, Every kingdom divided against itself is brought to desolation; and every city or house divided against itself shall not stand: And if Satan cast out Satan, he is divided against himself; how shall then his kingdom stand?"*
> *-- Matthew 12:25-26*

In particular, we as a congregation have often been assigned by the Lord to clearout the portals, which extend from our church into the area of God's throne in the third heaven. These were the portals that contained the gates and doors, which required all the fighting to work our way up through them. I cannot stress enough the importance of following God's leading in this area. Believe me, we do not sit around trying to think up some new battle to fight. In fact, we are often aware of demons, but because God has not told us to do anything against them, we just plead the blood of Jesus and leave them alone. However, when God says fight, WE FIGHT!

What does it feel like as you travel through a portal? As the angels take your spirit into these portals, you may feel a vibrating, pulsating sensation. I have also felt this happen as I entered different or new dimensions of the spirit. The angels taught me, as directed by the Lord, to go from one portal to another. We can pray, prophesy, and do spiritual warfare in them as well. There is a great amount of spiritual warfare that takes place in these various spiritual realms. By the way, it is absolutely necessary to be wearing our spiritual weapons on all missions. Two passages that have particular significance in this area are:

"And hath raised us up together, and made us sit together in heavenly places in Christ Jesus: ..."
-- *Ephesians 2:6*

"To the intent that now unto the principalities and powers in heavenly places might be known by the church the manifold wisdom of God, ..."
--*Ephesians 3:10*

[1] **Twilight of the Labyrinth,** by George Otis, Jr., Chosen Books, Grand Rapids, Michigan, 1997. (p. 90-91)
[2] **IBID** (p. 26-28)
[3] **Spiritual Warfare,** by Derek Prince, Whitaker House, 30 Hunt Valley Circle, New Kensington, Pennsylvania, 1987.
[4] **IBID**. (p. 21)

Chapter 9

JOINING THE FIGHT

"For we wrestle not against flesh and blood, but against principalities, against powers, against the rulers of the darkness of this world, against spiritual wickedness in high places."

-- *Ephesians 6:12*

One interesting thing I learned while going through certain gates had to do with authority. There were certain gates that required a specific rank of angel to enter. For example, I had successfully passed through one gate and was ready to advance to the next one when the angel that was with me told me that I would have to wait for another angel of higher rank to arrive before I could move on. The problem was that Pastor Crawford, my spiritual authority, was out of town and his permission was needed to gain the release of a higher-ranking angel. For the time being, the mission was put on hold.

As you will recall, in the heavenlies the angels are absolutely governed by the authority structures established by God. Even the dark angels operate under lines of authority established by God. In eons past, before Lucifer and one third of the angels rebelled against God, He established a hierarchy among the angels.

> *"For by him were all things created, that are in heaven, and that are in earth, visible and invisible, whether they be thrones, or dominions, or principalities, or powers: all things were created by him, and for him: ..."*
> *-- Colossians 1:16*

We know from scripture that Lucifer was an angel of the very highest angelic rank. There are not just two ranks of angels, the archangels and regular angels. Like a modern military organization, there are many ranks. Be very careful of the "celestial hierarchy" or "angelic hierarchy" lists you can find on the Internet, in books on angels or even in Bible software programs. These listings are not supported by scripture and are often contrary to scripture.

God's angels respect God's established authority levels, even among the ranks of fallen angels. By "respect," I do not mean they submit to or obey dark angels. I mean they recognize and defer to dark angels of a higher authority level than themselves. Godly angels will seek the help of higher-ranking angels in dealing with a dark angel of a higher rank. The scripture describes this in Daniel 10 where an angel was sent to deliver a message from God to Daniel.

> *"But the prince of the kingdom of Persia withstood me one and twenty days: but, lo, Michael, one of the chief princes, came to help me; and I remained there with the kings of Persia. ...Then said he, Knowest thou wherefore I come unto thee? and now will I return to fight with the prince of Persia: and when I am gone forth, lo, the prince of Grecia shall come."*
> *-- Daniel 10:13-20*

This explains why the mission was put on hold. The leading angel I was with was ranked lower than the dark angel guarding the gate. I had to wait a week for Pastor to return before the higher-ranking angel could be released to help me enter the gate. Once Pastor got back, we prayed and the angel was sent. The mission picked up right where we left off the week before.

Today, my Pastor is not aware moment by moment of everything the angels are doing with me. However, the Father gives him generalities so that He can cover me as my spiritual head. I have also made it a practice to check in with him and share important revelations or activities in which I am involved.

A person cannot just decide one day that they want to go traveling around in the portals. This type of spiritual activity must be initiated by God and overseen by His angels. I have never prayed to be taken into a portal. All I have asked the Lord to do is use me in any way He sees fit. For our church, the Lord sent me ahead to obtain keys to access these various gates so that I could give them to the saints who would follow me. Once the warfare was done at each gate and the keys were obtained, those in our church body were able to move quickly through with little or no resistance. Many of the portal highways in the second heaven require keys and codes to enter. There again, God will supply the believer with the keys and codes. The Lord willing, in a future book I will be sharing how keys and codes work.

As I went through the many gates and doors, working my way into the heavenlies, I could not help but think of the process, which the character named Christian had to undergo in **Pilgrim's Progress.**[1] It was very much a journey of exploration, and like the pilgrim, the Lord sent angelic guides along the way to help me.

87

The angels have also been of great assistance in the arena of warfare with the demonic. Even though they will fight for and with you, many times they are sent to simply train you to fight. I have faced off with various demonic forces with the Lord's angels at my side. In most instances I was required to do all the fighting. On many occasions, the angels would bring me incredible weapons with which to fight the enemy. Victories were won because I had the right weapon at the right time. Often the angels acted as referees to make sure the enemy did not take advantage of me.

In training us in spiritual warfare, the steps of our training and even the sequence in which lessons are learned are all ordered and orchestrated of the Lord. We each have an individualized goal or purpose in God's kingdom. The gifts, anointings, weapons, revelations and training experiences we receive from God are specific. They are designed to bring us to those places in time, ability and understanding wherein His perfect purposes will be fulfilled.

> *"Blessed be the LORD my strength, which teacheth my hands to war, and my fingers to fight: ..."*
> *-- Psalm 144:1*

We find the scriptures are filled with examples of the Lord God preparing and training His people to face and defeat their enemies. Remember how God sent the captain of the host of the Lord to give Joshua the battle strategy for taking the city of Jericho (Joshua 5:13-15)? God said He intentionally left heathen nations in the promise land to teach the new generation of Israel how to war.

"Now these are the nations which the LORD left, to prove Israel by them, even as many of Israel as had not known all the wars of Canaan; Only that the generations of the children of Israel might know, to teach them war, at the least such as before knew nothing thereof; ..."
                                        -- Judges 3:1-2

Paul charged Timothy to war.

"This charge I commit unto thee, son Timothy, according to the prophecies which went before on thee, that thou by them mightest war a good warfare; ..."
                                        -- 1 Timothy 1:18

I can remember that within a few weeks after our initial trip to Brownsville I was taken in the spirit by a couple of angels on a mission. I suddenly found myself in someone's house where the angels set me down, and as I watched they went through the house looking for demons. The angels fought and defeated the demons. After the house was clean, they took me back to the church.

When the Lord takes us on a mission into the spirit realm, it will almost always entail learning a valuable lesson. Obviously our faith is strengthened each time we accept the invitation of the Lord to be taken on a mission. As believers, we must learn how to trust in the Lord to take care of us and to supply any weapons we may need. In addition, we need to learn to listen to the voice of the Holy Spirit as He directs us in what we are to do. Very similarly, we learn to listen to the angels as they give us necessary information about what we are to face and what our response should be.

The Lord is revealing many of the operations of the angelic hosts. They do not just fly around all day and sing. All angels have specific job functions. Just like humans they have purpose. Remember angels are not omniscient, but the angels know of the enemy's every movement. One discovery that surprised me was that there are areas in heaven with high-tech equipment that monitors the enemy. I was amazed at how some of our present day surveillance equipment bears a resemblance to this heavenly equipment. It will not be long until the body of Christ steps into their heavenly places and starts accessing some of this very strategic information. It will cause us to operate in a word of knowledge at a level that we could never have imagined. We see that Elisha operated at this strategic word of knowledge level.

> *"Then the king of Syria warred against Israel, and took counsel with his servants, saying, In such and such a place shall be my camp. And the man of God sent unto the king of Israel, saying, Beware that thou pass not such a place; for thither the Syrians are come down. And the king of Israel sent to the place which the man of God told him and warned him of, and saved himself there, not once nor twice. Therefore the heart of the king of Syria was sore troubled for this thing; and he called his servants, and said unto them, Will ye not shew me which of us is for the king of Israel? And one of his servants said, None, my lord, O king: but Elisha, the prophet that is in Israel, telleth the king of Israel the words that thou speakest in thy bedchamber."*
> *-- 2 Kings 6:8-12*

The Lord wants His Church to step into a "knowing" that will paralyze the enemy. God is going to draw us into a place in Him where we will know the enemy's attack plans at their initiation point. Until now, the church has generally reacted to what the enemy is doing. We have no idea where he is going to strike and, in fact, the enemy seems to know what we are going to do before we do it! Let me remind you, the enemy is not omniscient either! However, he does have ways of intercepting answers to prayers and learning our plans (See Daniel 10). God promises this kind of revelatory knowledge to His children as well.

> *"For there is nothing covered, that shall not be revealed; neither hid, that shall not be known. Therefore whatsoever ye have spoken in darkness shall be heard in the light; and that which ye have spoken in the ear in closets shall be proclaimed upon the housetops."*
>
> *-- Luke 12:2-3*

How can we step into a greater "knowing"? It all begins by taking our seats, our heavenly places in Christ Jesus. This is not just for after we die and go to heaven. Our heavenly seats are waiting for us NOW! As we begin our ministry in these heavenly places, we will understand more about the technical operation of the angels. As we learn from angels about where the enemy's strongholds are and what is the most effective way of bringing them down, we will begin delivering severe blows to the enemy.

The enemy has ways of finding out many of the purposes of God and convenes demonic councils to develop strategies to hinder them. However, we have basically never bothered to press in and find out what the enemy has planned in retaliation. Many saints will be sent by the Lord as spies to listen in on the councils of the enemy. We will obtain information about the enemy's plans and be able to pray and intercede accordingly. We will cause great confusion in the ranks of the enemy. Elisha did just that.

God is allowing His children to use many of the resources that have until now been available primarily to His angels. Our enemy has his own information resources, and those on earth who pay the high price of serving Satan are able to use them. The demons relay this information through mediums, psychics, card readers, astrologers, seances and many other less obvious methods. The enemy has stolen knowledge that should never have been made available to his followers. Sadly, through ignorance and apathy, the church has turned away from the knowledge God wants her to have in order to defeat Satan. The church has never truly stepped into her place in the heavenlies and attained the things God has prepared for her. Therefore, she has not been able to make the significant onslaught of the enemy's kingdom God intends for her to make.

Satan has deceived the church into believing that her rightful position and focus is here on earth. Satan has not had to worry about protecting his kingdom's headquarters in the second heaven. Since very few Christians have moved into the spiritual authority of their heavenly seats, he has not been challenged there. We have lacked the supernatural knowledge and the weapons that God has fashioned for us. More importantly, we have lacked the passion for the Father's heart that is necessary in order to take our rightful seats in these heavenly places.

You cannot really know the Lord and how awesome He is until you have been seated with Him in heavenly places. Why are we just now hearing about this? It is in the Word...it has been there all the time. We have just been too blinded by the lust of the flesh, the lust of the eyes and the pride of life to see it. Now, the Lord is making it painfully obvious to the church, because of what is just ahead, the final hours of the end times!

Without going into great detail at this juncture, suffice it to say that the level of evil on this planet will swell very soon. When this time comes, if a believer has not stepped into their rightful authority in the "heavenly places," they will face incredible danger. The Lord warns us in Matthew 24 of the worldwide deception that is coming. Many of the "wars and rumors of war" will be those that are fought in the spirit realm. I am not trying to sound fatalistic or cause panic but I know that the Lord desires for His children to step into their places of authority and fight.

I am so grateful to the Lord for the preparation He has been giving us. I am thrilled that as I move in the spirit realm I am not attacked as fiercely or frequently as before. As we begin ruling from our heavenly place in Christ Jesus, the enemy is more cautious about taking careless shots at us. He knows that we have the authority to deal with him. He knows that we carry weapons that can destroy him. Whether you agree that we should be fighting or not, please consider asking God to bring you into your place of rulership in Him. God is waiting for His saints to join with the heavens in declaring His glory.

> *"The heavens declare the glory of God; and the firmament sheweth his handywork."*
> *-- Psalm 19:1*

As I mentioned before, I was attacked, stabbed or strangled on many occasions when my spirit was on various missions with the angels. However, as I gained authority in the spirit, partly by my willing participation and partly by winning battles, the attacks had less effect on me. In the early attacks, though they occurred in the spirit, I could still feel the pain in my body. In time I was fortified with armor and weapons that all but stopped the pain caused by these attacks. I then began inflicting great pain and destruction in the enemy's camp.

> *"For we wrestle not against flesh and blood, but against principalities, against powers, against the rulers of the darkness of this world, against spiritual wickedness in high places."*
> -- *Ephesians 6:12*

On one mission in December of 1998, I was taken into a different kind of portal. I saw two horrific looking demons. This was a very evil area and I felt overwhelmed by it. There were angels with me, and I was handed a sword to use to battle through this portal. It took some time but we made it through. At the end of the battle, there was a great celebration and I was told I had passed a test. I was then taken to heaven and after being honored, I gave to Jesus the spoils acquired during the battle. Something was then placed inside of me.

Besides learning how to do battle with the enemy, the process God took our intercessors through taught us how to work with the angels. The angels are each so different. Many of the ones assigned to me during the battles in the second heaven were warring angels. I learned to trust their words and admonitions because they were the words of the Lord. Often ministering angels were sent to minister encouragement and strength after particularly violent encounters with the enemy. On some occasions, angels who were anointed for praise and worship were sent to help lift our spirits. What a time of rejoicing! These times were my favorite.

With almost every victory won, I received some kind of anointing or gift from the Lord delivered by His angels. There were several times that I received crowns, a robe, rings and several swords. For some reason I was given many swords of various sizes and degrees of ornateness. (I have since learned these swords represent revelations of God's truth that can be used as weapons against the enemy.) Many times indescribable things were put into my spirit.

> *"And I said, Let them [angels] set a fair mitre [diadem] upon his head. So they set a fair mitre upon his head, and clothed him with garments. And the angel of the LORD stood by."*
> *-- Zechariah 3:5*

I know that some people have to see things with their eyes in order to believe. It is hard to prove what God has done in your spirit. However, I have been amazed by the confirmations of those with a seer gifting, as they describe the anointings and the weapons that I know are on my spirit.

If things were not incredible enough already, the angels have been bringing specially crafted, high-tech weapons for this hour. These weapons are very unusual and sophisticated; some are used to paralyze the enemy while others destroy him. God is also equipping us with devices designed originally for the angels. These include devices that aid in communicating with angels and other equipment that allow us to be cloaked or hidden from the enemy.

> *"For in the time of trouble he shall hide me in his pavilion: in the secret of his tabernacle shall he hide me; he shall set me up upon a rock."*
> *-- Psalm 27:5*

I have learned to live in a state of readiness. When I come out of a powerful time of intercession, I know there is a good chance I am going to get blasted by the enemy. Many of these attacks are experienced not only individually but also corporately. Over and over again, we find that Satan will launch a series of identical attacks against various members of our congregation simultaneously. We have a weekly time when we actually review with our intercessors what the current enemy strategy is against us. For example, one time it was the thought that "I am the only one under attack. I had better keep it quiet or everyone else will know I am not really that spiritual." Once it was brought into the open as an attack, almost every single person spoke up and said, "Hey! That is what I have been struggling with this week!" Demonic spirits such as Jezebel, Absalom, Belial and Beelzebub have attacked us continually. Invariably the attacks on our church come against the leadership first or are focused on attacking the authority of the leadership.

---

[1] **Pilgrim's Progress**, by John Bunyan, Fleming H. Revell Publisher, Grand Rapids, Michigan, 1688 edition 11.

Chapter 10

THE IMPORTANCE OF DISCERNMENT

"But strong meat belongeth to them that are of full age, even those who by reason of use have their senses exercised to discern both good and evil."

-- Hebrews 5:14

There will be many that say it is not safe to be ministering with angels. They may feel there is too much risk of a person hearing from a demon rather than one of the Lord's angels. Believe me, this argument comes directly from Satan himself. After all, the enemy wants to make sure we find some excuse not to step into this ministry. Satan will do everything he can to discourage us or cause us to fear this ministry.

When the Lord began opening up the angelic realm to me, I was very unsure and a little fearful. I was not sure I was supposed to be allowing these kinds of encounters to happen. However, the Holy Spirit encouraged me and gave me a wonderful peace about what I was experiencing, while at the same time anointing me with an incredible discernment. He began giving me wisdom to know whether the enemy was involved in a situation or not and taught me that there is nothing to fear because He is in complete charge of everything. As long as we stay in obedience and submission to the Lord and our God-given authorities, we will be completely protected. However, those who walk in rebellion will not have angelic encounters but could very well have demonic encounters.

With these things in mind, the first step in preparing for angelic visitations from the Lord is to ask the Lord for the gift of discerning of spirits. One of the best books on discernment that I have found is Sharpen Your Discernment, by Roberts Liardon.[1] In our Saints in Training School, we have two courses on discernment that students are required to take before they can enroll in our class on **Ministering with Angels**.

I would suggest contacting our church at www.thefatherschurch.org or (214) 821-5290 for more information about our discernment courses if you have any questions.

The following are a few helpful pointers that will help to increase your spiritual discernment. First, God is in control and desires to give you the necessary discernment so you will not be deceived. Second, we must ask God for the anointing for discernment. Finally, we must do the things He asks us to do in order to allow discernment to be activated in our spiritual walk with Him. DISCERNMENT MUST BE PRACTICED.

> *"But strong meat belongeth to them that are of full age, even those who by reason of use have their senses exercised to discern both good and evil."*
> *-- Hebrews 5:14*

Our course on spiritual discernment is a very practical, not theoretical teaching. We have found Liardon's book to be invaluable for this kind of instruction. The students must also write a paper on <u>Commitment To Conquer,</u> by Bob Beckett.[2] Beckett's book takes discernment to a broader spectrum. God wants us to be able to discern on a personal level as well as on a societal level. Most importantly, we study the book of Nehemiah that provides some wonderful insights on discernment.

After the class received a certain level of instruction on the gift of discerning of spirits, they were asked to go to a local bookstore. The Lord told me specifically which bookstore to send them to and said that He was going to activate the student's discernment while they were there. The students were asked to write down what they sensed as they walked through this huge bookstore no matter how insignificant the response might seem to them. This particular bookstore is full of many demonic influences, everything from new age to witchcraft. Many of the students experienced a discerning of evil influences for the very first time; with some having physical reactions to the presence of the demons. There were several that felt the demons following them as they walked around the store. Some experienced pains in different places in their body, while others felt nauseated. Everyone is different in their reaction in discerning evil spirits. The important thing is to learn what God does to alert you to the fact that there are demonic forces in an area.

In the second course on discernment, the students were put into teams of four to five people and assigned specific areas of our city in order to discern the demonic activity at work in that area. Once again, God was faithful to show the different teams the strongholds of the enemy. Several saw demons and demonic structures in the spirit realm. One group saw demons disappear into the ground as they drove into the area.

The Lord taught us to discern both the angelic and the demonic realms. Why? I believe it was because He does not want us to be deceived. He knows that the enemy will come to deceive us, presenting himself as an angel of light. Scripture says, *"our senses exercised to discern both good and evil."* Our focus is the pursuit of the kingdom of God. God will give us the necessary discernment to recognize the counterfeit anointings of the enemy. He also gives us the proof-text for whether we are dealing with an angel of God or an angel of darkness.

> *"Hereby know ye the Spirit of God: Every spirit that confesseth that Jesus Christ is come in the flesh is of God: And <u>every spirit that confesseth not that Jesus Christ is come in the flesh is not of God</u>: and this is that spirit of antichrist, whereof ye have heard that it should come; and even now already is it in the world."*
>
> -- 1 John 4:2-3

Believe me, this scripture works! If I have any doubt at all whether I am talking to an angel of God or not, I ask this question, "Can you confess that Jesus Christ has come in the flesh?" The angels of the Lord begin rejoicing and the angels of darkness usually leave quickly or try to change the subject without answering the question. Believe the Word! Some still wonder, "What if they do not answer, what will I do?" The Lord's angels WILL answer. We must trust the Lord on this issue.

Not everyone will move at the same pace in learning how to discern. Some will be more gifted right away while for others it may take some time. However, I believe God intends for ALL of His children to be able to discern with more clarity and more accuracy. In Matthew 24, Jesus warns his disciples about the coming deceptions upon the earth. These deceptions will increase during the end times.

"And Jesus answered and said unto them, Take heed that no man deceive you."
                                    -- Matthew 24:4

The only way not to be deceived is to know the truth. To know the truth we must be able to discern precisely. Even if you decide not to discern the angels, at least allow the Holy Spirit to teach you to discern the activity of the enemy.

God wants ALL His children to move mightily in the discerning of spirits. We have to move beyond just getting "weird vibes" about people to knowing what spirit is influencing or attacking the individual. What spirits do we need to be able to discern? There are evil spirits, angelic spirits, human spirits, and the Spirit of the Lord. We need to be able to discern good and evil. By the way, most of our students do not see demons but perceive them.

After the Lord taught us how to recognize the presence of demons, He then taught us to recognize the presence of angels. The Lord assigned angels to begin training us how to minister with them. When this starts happening in your church, the effect will be incredible!

---

[1] **Sharpen Your Discernment**, by Roberts Liardon, Albury Publishing, Tulsa, Oklahoma, 1997.
[2] **Commitment To Conquer**, by Bob Beckett, Chosen Books, Grand Rapid, Michigan, 1997.

Chapter 11

ANGELIC ACTIVATIONS

"And though the Lord give you the bread of adversity, and the water of affliction, yet shall not thy teachers be removed into a corner any more, but thine eyes shall see thy teachers: And thine ears shall hear a word behind thee, saying, This is the way, walk ye in it, when ye turn to the right hand, and when ye turn to the left."

-- Isaiah 30:20-21

Before I continue in sharing how the Lord taught us to minister with angels, there are a few facts that everyone needs to know about the Lord's angels. I have cited a few scriptural examples. There are many, many more.

Angels have emotions. They rejoice over the salvation of each person (Luke 15:10).

Angels bring messages and gifts. The word "angel" in both the Hebrew and the Greek means "messenger" (Zechariah 3:3-5, Luke 1:11-21; Acts 10:3-7).

Angels serve the Lord and are sent to "minister for them who shall be heirs of salvation" (Hebrews 1:14).

There is rank and order among the angels (Daniel 10:10-21).

Angels have purpose (Hebrews 1:7).

While scripture never specifically addresses the gender of angels, it does use masculine names and pronouns. The secular practice of depicting angels as feminine, soft, pretty and accommodating is very deceptive. Angels are mighty, powerful and come with purpose and wisdom. They are not trying to earn their wings nor are they doing good deeds in hopes of making it into heaven.

There are too many people, including Christians, who believe angels are here only to rescue us from disastrous situations. Most people have a "guardian angel" mentality that limits the extent of what they believe angels do. If we will only listen and participate with His plan, God is releasing His angels to have greater interaction with His children in this hour. There are incredible prospects ahead as we enter into this partnership with the Lord and His angels. As more and more saints experience angelic interactions, less strangeness will be attached to these encounters. I hope you will be one to step out of the boat and enter into this incredible dimension of God's kingdom.

When the Lord told me He wanted me to teach a course on ministering with angels, I had many questions for Him. How was I supposed to pull this off? What was I to do if the people rejected this teaching? The Lord told me not to worry about what people would think or say about the course, just to do it and leave the results to Him. The Lord had me draw from the things He had taught me personally and teach them to the class following very specific directions.

Before I actually started teaching the course, the Lord had me select eight students and do an angelic activation with each of them. I simply prayed that God would open their spirits to the angelic realm. God was more than faithful to reveal His angels. It was awesome as the angels came and ministered to them. Almost every one perceived angels, several had conversations with angels, and some saw angels for the first time. Others began having angelic visitations at work and home. It was incredible to see these things happening with others.

When I started the actual course, these eight individuals became captains over teams of 4-5 people. The captains would meet with their teams and ask the Lord to send the angels to them, and the Lord did. Each group participated in approximately five activations. The individuals in each group had varying encounters with the angels. Students journalized the encounters they had in both their group activations and in their personal prayer times. Here are a few excerpts from their journals.

> *During this activation I sensed angels walking with me. This time there were three. All of them were behind me. I understood that each one of them walked with me in separate spiritual arenas. One was here in this realm, one was in the realm of heaven in which warfare takes place, and the third walks with me in the throne room. Each had characteristics that were representative of the realm they minister in. The throne room representative wore garments for worship. The warring angel had much armor and the other just seemed to watch everything surrounding me.*

-- A.D., Dallas, Texas

Came in about 5 minutes late! Started praying and had a very good prayer time! I knew the angels were here - their presence was evident. I had an image of a very large angel with curly blonde hair with eyes that were drawing (pure, loving, but powerful.) probably 3 or 4 times taller than a man -- maybe 20 - 25 ft.

Nothing was said - I just saw him standing in the altar area in front of the pulpit - looking down at our team!

-- K.M., Garland, Texas

As I climbed the stairs to one of our prayer rooms, I was made aware that an angel was climbing with me. Stepping into the room, immediately a conversation began between the two of us. This conversation lasted from half an hour to maybe a full hour. I am just not sure.

I wish I would have written everything down, but at the time I did not want to stop the conversation. I do remember some of the things and will try to briefly relate them below.

1. *He told me his name is Jerome -- he also said, "I stand beside Michael the Archangel."*
2. *He had recently been assigned to me.*
3. *He told me he would respond to those things that pertain to me and to the Father's purpose.*
4. *He is assigned to instruct me, protect me and keep the enemy from preventing God's purposes from being fulfilled.*

5. I asked him if he was ALWAYS with me. His response was, that he goes here and there (pointing in different directions). He was ever aware of my state and that he flies like the lightening at the command of the Almighty (to aid me).

6. He instructed me to say nothing <u>more</u> and nothing <u>less</u> than what I heard and/or saw. Everything will be very specific and purposed for individual circumstances and people.

7. He said that the angels enjoy looking into the things of men and the "happenings" to the heirs of salvation. They also enjoy seeing us share love one for another because this pleases the Lord.

8. He instructed me to follow him around the room. (This seemed strange to me but I could see where he was walking so I simply obeyed and followed him.)

This entire time and conversation was so very natural -- it did not seem strange to me. Now, that <u>IS</u> strange.

-- J.V., Dallas, Texas

As I walked into the sanctuary I sensed an anointing. As I was standing, I sensed an angel by me and my tongues changed to a high pitched language, also my body was shifting from side to side. As we moved into a group my language got even faster and the shifting from side to side continued and also leaning forward as to almost fall over. This continued through the whole activation. Then an angel began to speak to me. This is what he said; "The Lord is preparing you for great things. You have the song of the Lord in you. Sing unto the Father!" He went on to say that I am swimming in murky waters and I

*was just about to reach the clear waters of the Lord. He told
me to hang onto the Father. Give 100% to him, not 99%.*

-- R.M., Garland, Texas

*I arrived a few minutes early and Paul was already in
the balcony in deep prayer and angelic activity. I knew in my
spirit that there was a presence of the heavenly host. I climbed
the stairs and opened the door and Paul directed me to sit down
on the pew where he had been sitting.*

*When I did, an angel sitting on my right, which I had
contact with on previous Wednesdays, told me to hold his hand.
He kept saying to take the hand(s) and I thought hands, I am
holding your hand. I stood up and reached for his other hand
and had a faint visual outline of him standing in front of me
holding my hands. The angel seemed to be about seven feet tall
and overshadowed me with his presence. I was not fearful or
afraid but waited in expectancy to receive what he had to say.*

*He told me to take off my shoes. I asked him why and
he said I was standing on holy ground. I then replied quite
humbly that I was in the balcony. He then responded, "You are
standing in heavenly places in the spirit."*

*My hands were tingling and had an electricity
sensation. I know I was receiving an impartation. He said that
this sensation was for physical healing as well as for healings of
the heart, which I interpreted to mean emotional and
psychological hurts and woundings.*

*He then asked me to touch the other angels hands that
were standing around him. One of the other intercessors came
and prayed by me and later shared that angels were*

surrounding me. I knew there were at least five other angels, including the angel I communed with. I did not feel anything when I reached out in faith to touch their hands. I was interrupted in this process by Paul asking us to gather for closing prayer as it was almost seven o'clock. Again the time had slipped quickly away.

During the entire activation, I was speaking in divers tongues. I was always cognizant of my surroundings but would easily become lost in the spirit and then slip back to reality. This process repeated again and again. During certain periods of time, the voices of the other intercessors present would rise in a uniform chorus of voices together and then subside. I at one point asked how many angels were present and the angel said one for each person and a multitude of others in the area.

-- T. S., Dallas, Texas

Tonight was awesome. We had such unity and agreement in the Spirit. You could distinctly sense the incoming of the angels. My spirit leaped right into heaven. At the same time different manifestations occurred in the other team members. Our tongues lifted, got stronger, more forceful and very creative. There was a very real presence. We stepped into a new dimension of faith, you could feel it. There was an excitement and confidence I had not had.

Just when we thought we might be done, one of the pastors came up. You could instantly feel the increase in authority and the power of the angelic company with him. They evidently had something for each of us through the prayer of our pastor. As he prayed for each of us, the deposit from the

Spirit was different for each one, but distinctly what the Lord had for us at that time. In addition, what was brought from the Lord was a seal on the new level of faith He had taken us to.

-- M.T., Dallas, Texas

We were instructed to find and join with someone and go to a place in the balcony and to pray out loud in the spirit and see what would happen. So J.P. and I paired up and went to the top corner.

I noticed after a short time that the tongues flowing out of me were changing, perhaps once or twice. Then I felt this rhyme and spontaneous melody flowing. So I went with it. I felt that an angel was with me and leading me in a simple happy childlike melody of praise to the Lord. This was fun. This is when I was called by Pastor Paul and asked to walk into where the angel was standing. So I did. As I walked in, I felt a shooting upwards of my spirit. As if I had entered a tunnel that only traveled upwards in a flurry of power and glory. It was pretty wild. Something I had never experienced.

-- I.H., Dallas, Texas

Once the initial activations took place, the students were to expect angels to come and minister to them at any time. The angels are helping familiarize us with the spirit realm. During the activations the angels brought gifts and anointings for the students, or simply had a conversation. There were varying accounts of what each student perceived that the angels were doing during these activations. Yet without discussing it among themselves, student after student would describe virtually the same thing.

Basically the Lord provided at least one angel per person in each group. Some of the angels, once assigned to an individual, stayed with them for the duration of these activations. The Lord said for us to continue to be sensitive, as He would continue to give us more training with the angels. These activations are not an end unto themselves. They merely provide a safe framework to launch a believer into ministering with angels. God is determined for His children and His angels to work together for His kingdom to come here on earth.

As I stated earlier, the angels work within the framework of the authority structure in each church. I am under the leadership of our senior pastor. He has given me the authority to operate in this somewhat unique ministry. The angels were released to the captains as they submitted to my authority. Then when the captains prayed for their individual groups, the angels were released to work with their group members. As you can see, this particular ministry absolutely requires submission on all levels.

Under no circumstance can a captain, a group member, or even I, myself initiate angelic activations on our own. In other words, the activations must flow from the head of the church. The pastor or spiritual head of your church must initiate this ministry. The angels will not work in a rebellious environment. They are required by God to respect the authority that is in a church, even if those in authority choose not to pursue the kingdom of God in this manner.

Can I come to a local church and help them launch into the angelic realm? Yes, but only if the leaders are in agreement. Otherwise, God would have to contradict everything He has taught us in the Word about authority. I am not saying that individual members or certain leaders

111

will not have angelic encounters. God works in individual lives in His own sovereign way. But if the corporate body of a church wants to move as a whole into this ministry and experience this facet of the kingdom of God on a regular basis, they must submit to God's process.

Chapter 12

COUNTING THE COST

"If any man come to me, and hate not his father, and mother, and wife, and children, and brethren, and sisters, yea, and his own life also, he cannot be my disciple. And whosoever doth not bear his cross, and come after me, cannot be my disciple. For which of you, intending to build a tower, sitteth not down first, and counteth the cost, whether he have sufficient to finish it? Lest haply, after he hath laid the foundation, and is not able to finish it, all that behold it begin to mock him, Saying, This man began to build, and was not able to finish. ... So likewise, whosoever he be of you that forsaketh not all that he hath, he cannot be my disciple."

-- Luke 14:26-33

I would like to reemphasize that God's process starts with His leaders. My senior pastor and I have been through the most incredible testing and refining. Once we thought He was finished, God would bring more refinement. We have learned that this is a life-long process that requires a day by day intimate relationship with God. God is not going to trust untested or unproven vessels with this great responsibility.

God wants people who are totally committed to Him. If your church is full of good people who pay tithes, that is not enough. If your members

113

have been Christians for 30 years or more, that is not enough. God is looking for a church that will pay the price. One that will die to its programs and traditions and as a corporate body chase hard after the heart of the Father. We are talking about wholesale changes, stopping everything and focusing on finding out what God has purposed for your church.

The biggest challenge for many pastors will come from their board members or elders. You must realize that everyone will not run to embrace this ministry. When the enemy comes to cause division and strife within your church, as pastors and leaders you quickly learn how strong you are in the spirit, and how determined you are to allow God's kingdom to come.

God was not pleased with how we were conducting our church. He did not think we needed all of the wonderful programs we provided. God had a list of changes He wanted us to make, and at the top of the list was a focus on prayer and worship. God's priorities for our church were the first area of attack the enemy used to cause strife and division.

Nevertheless, when you stand before His throne and try to tell Him how impossible these drastic changes are to make, do not look for sympathy. God does not like excuses! The Holy Father will judge your heart and your desires and find you lacking. He wants you pursuing Him wholeheartedly.

What if the leadership desires to pursue God's priorities but the people do not? It is decision time! Our decision cost us two-thirds of our congregation over a four-year span. However, today we are unified and have one basic focus...the heart of the Father. We have no other goals in our church. We have an evangelism outreach, but it has undergone modifications called for by the Father. We minister to our children and youth, but now instead of entertainment we lead them to intimacy with the Father. We teach them prayer, evangelism, discernment, and ministering with angels. God wants our programs to have His handprint on them. The various departments in our church function as part of the whole, supporting God's purpose for our church. Our children and youth are learning how to flow in the things of the kingdom of God just like the adults.

God wants to relate to the local church in a more direct fashion. Some churches model themselves after another church or function as a puppet of a larger organization. God wants to speak directly to the pastor of each and every church and reveal His priorities for that specific body of believers. He is calling His Church to His heart. God wants to govern every individual congregation Himself, and His priorities outweigh denominational structures.

Every church needs to evaluate its present course. Is your church directed by different programs, members' preferences and traditions or by God? Once you answer this question, then ask God what needs to be done to get on course. This will require your congregation to fast and pray about what needs to be done.

The Lord does not want the church to continue with business as usual. Christ desperately wants His bride to have her ear to His heart. He wants to transform our churches and give us new wineskins.

> *"Neither do men put new wine into old bottles: else the bottles break, and the wine runneth out, and the bottles perish: but they put new wine into new bottles, and both are preserved."*
>
> *-- Matthew 9:17*

Both churches and individuals are required to get rid of the old to get ready for the new. As we become prophetic churches, we will not only hear His purposes but also declare them.

There are many churches that will enter into this deeper dimension of the kingdom of God. God has been speaking to some of you pastors already. Others of you will hear from God very soon, in fact, some of you are hearing His voice even as you read these words. What your church needs to do is begin praying and seeking the Lord with renewed passion. This is God's perfect time.

Neither our church nor its leaders are interested in gaining a following. God's revealed purpose for us is to be a catalyst encouraging saints around the globe to step into the fullness of the kingdom of God. Can what God has accomplished in our church be attained in yours as well? YES! We willingly offer you our help and prayers. Every church must still pursue His purpose for themselves. Your church's calling will probably be different than our calling. The thing we will have in common though, will be seeking His heart and His will alone, and not man's.

Chapter 13

A "TYPICAL" SERVICE?

"Are they not all ministering spirits, sent forth to minister for them who shall be heirs of salvation?"
-- Hebrews 1:14

To what extent can we expect angels to be involved in our lives and ministries? One of the great healing evangelists of the 1930's - 1950's was William Branham. Branham had incredible experiences ministering with angels. His healing services were characterized by angelic visitations. He would talk until God's angel showed up and then he would begin praying for people under a powerful prophetic/healing anointing. The angel would tell him vital information (words of knowledge) about people to whom he was ministering. Sometimes, Branham would have visions while ministering to people. Similarly, I have found that when angels are around, both words of knowledge and visual revelations increase. Branham is only one of many great men and women of God who have ministered with angels. Kathryn Kuhlman, John G. Lake[1], Maria Woodworth-Etter[2] and others also moved in this amazing power ministry.

117

I believe these angelic anointings will soon influence both worship and preaching. In worship, we will hear singers' voices taken to a new level of excellence. Angels could bring to those with no singing ability the anointing to sound like one who has great talent and training. Angels who have anointings in instrumentation will bring these anointings to those who have never touched a musical instrument.[3]

In preaching, we could be in for some real excitement. The angels have incredible skill when it comes to preaching. The preaching style could change from service to service depending on the specific angel sent with the message for that service. Can an angel's influence be manifested in this way? Yes it can, perhaps you have never noticed the verse of scripture that speaks of angels preaching.

> *"And I saw another angel fly in the midst of heaven, having the everlasting gospel to preach unto them that dwell on the earth, and to every nation, and kindred, and tongue, and people, ..."*
>
> *-- Revelation 14:6*

Not only will the preaching itself be taken to new levels of anointing, but the results will be incredible. As we preach, the angels will begin moving throughout the congregation and ministering to the people. An angel may get the attention of the minister and tell him/her the Lord is ready to heal or deliver someone. As the anointed words come out of the minister's mouth or as musicians play anointed sounds – miracles will happen. This is teamwork of the greatest kind and only requires our cooperation with the angels. It will be impossible to predict how services are going to flow.

"The wind bloweth where it listeth, and thou hearest the sound thereof, but canst not tell whence it cometh, and whither it goeth: so is every one that is born of the Spirit."
-- John 3:8

In a crusade, each service could be totally distinct from the one before as different angels are sent. With the Holy Spirit directing the angelic and those in charge of the service humbly allowing Him complete control, the most awesome, not-of–this-world miracles and displays of God's glory can be expected. Ministers will become facilitators as they direct the audience in cooperating with what the angels have been released to do. What about the laying on of hands (Hebrews 6:2)? Yes, this will still take place, but with huge crowds forming where the Holy Spirit is moving like this, it will take the help of a supernatural ministry team to handle all those that need a touch. Jesus did not lay hands on everyone He healed. Peter's shadow was so anointed that those that stepped into it were healed (Matthew 8:13, Acts 5:15).

When we completely allow the Holy Spirit to take control of our temples, look out! All kinds of things are liable to happen.

"What? know ye not that your body is the temple of the Holy Ghost which is in you, which ye have of God, and ye are not your own?"
--1 Corinthians 6:19

Paul the Apostle said, *"we die daily"* (1 Corinthians 15:31). He was not talking about his spirit nor was he talking about his physical body; he was talking about his soul. Within the make-up of the soul is our will that can accept or reject the influence of the Holy Spirit. Therefore, we can also accept or reject the influence of the angels sent from the Holy Spirit. God's purpose is for the Holy Spirit to be in complete control of

119

us. You may be thinking about 1 Corinthians 14:32 that says, *"And the spirits of the prophets are subject to the prophets."* This is correct and we are always conscious of what the Holy Spirit is doing in and through us. We can stop the working of the Holy Spirit since He does not "take over" our spirits. We are not puppets. We may not understand what He is doing or be able to put the right words together to explain it, but we must learn to cooperate with the Holy Spirit. We can willingly give our spirits to the control of the Holy Spirit and let Him direct us or we can maintain personal control and resist the moving of the Holy Spirit in our lives.

When the preaching anointing hit the Apostle Peter on the Day of Pentecost, he became like another man. He preached with incredible power and authority. He spoke as a man who had rabbinical training. Peter could not do what he was doing in the natural, but with the supernatural help of the Holy Spirit he rose above his natural abilities and limitations. As a result, three thousand people were saved after his first "anointed" sermon.

If these anointings stay true to form, as in intercession, the supernatural abilities will come suddenly and then leave with the departure of the angel. The story of Samson helps to illustrate this facet of being under an anointing. Samson's strength would come on him suddenly; and after a great feat for God, Samson would again be as any other man. Some ministers might arrogantly think this anointing to preach is a gift of their own and not realize an angel is assisting them. Be careful though, God will not share His glory. Humility is key to ministering anything of lasting value in God's kingdom. This is especially true of ministering with angels.

[1] **John G. Lake, His Life, His Sermons, His Boldness of Faith,** Kenneth Copeland Publications Fort Worth, Texas 1994. (p. 139-140)

[2] **Signs and Wonders**, by Maria Woodworth-Etter, Whitaker House, 1997. (p. 350-351, 433)

[3] **John G. Lake, His Life, His Sermons, His Boldness of Faith**, Kenneth Copeland Publications, Fort Worth, Texas, 1994. (p. 43-45)

Chapter 14

PROPHETIC WORDS

"But the word of the LORD was unto them precept upon precept, precept upon precept; line upon line, line upon line; here a little, and there a little."

-- Isaiah 28:13

We must be cautious not to limit our beliefs about end-time events to books written in past generations. Throughout history God has revealed Himself and His plans little by little. One reason I believe this so strongly is because every generation of Bible teachers has had a different understanding and explanation of what the last days will be like. The Lord told me they would not be anything like what has been taught and depicted by many. Paul the Apostle, John the Beloved and Peter all speak of God continuing to reveal things not understood in times past to the church in these last days.

"And he said, Go thy way, Daniel: for the words are closed up and sealed till the time of the end. Many shall be purified, and made white, and tried; but the wicked shall do wickedly: and none of the wicked shall understand; but the wise shall understand."

-- Daniel 12:9-10

This is not intended as a slam on those who have special expertise in end-time prophecy. All this means is that we had better listen for the Lord to tell us day by day what is to come. The books of Daniel and Revelation do not explain to us all the details of the complete picture. God will reveal the details contained within these prophetic scriptures in His perfect timing. For us to trust men's assumptions, just because we want to have it all figured out is ludicrous.

> *"Even the <u>mystery which hath been hid</u> from ages and from generations, but <u>now is made manifest</u> to his saints: ..."*
> *-- Colossians 1:26*

The Lord will bring clarity to previously misunderstood passages of scripture. What God does not want is our human head knowledge or best guess. This will not suffice. We must contend for the fresh revelation of truth the Holy Spirit will be bringing.

Peter speaks of present truth, meaning the truth that God is presently revealing to the church. For example, at the beginning of the twentieth century, God began revealing the 2000 year-old truth about speaking in tongues. It was not "new" truth but it was present truth. I could give you many other examples in the past 100-years of things that have been in the Word of God all along, but which only recently became understood, believed, and put into practice. Ministering with angels is present truth for today.

> *"Wherefore I will not be negligent to put you always in remembrance of these things, though ye know them, and be established in the present truth."*
> *-- 2 Peter 1:12*

God is about to blow the gasket off our traditions and narrow-minded thinking. Americans, especially churchgoers, are very opinionated. Multitudes of congregations say they want a fresh move of God; however, they only welcome it if God stays within the parameters of their comfort zones.

For years, the corporate body of Christ has been praying for the kingdom of God to come. It will be interesting as His kingdom comes into churches all over the world to see if they will indeed embrace it. We know from scripture that God's ways and thoughts are totally different from ours.

> *"For my thoughts are not your thoughts, neither are your ways my ways, saith the Lord. [9] For as the heavens are higher than the earth, so are my ways higher than your ways, and my thoughts than your thoughts."*
> *-- Isaiah 55:8-9*

We cannot ask God to come down and visit us with His manifest presence and expect to feel comfortable. This is not possible! If you want God that means you must want His kingdom, too. In the kingdom of God, the angels come first to prepare the place for His presence to dwell. This alone will stretch your conception of how God operates. For example, most of the angels come and go, but God has stationed certain angels in our church for several years now. You will face an even greater challenge when elders, patriarchs and saints of ages past begin to appear. As different aspects of heaven are established in your church, your understanding of the working of God's kingdom is expanded.

The angels will be instrumental in deliverance ministry. I understand now what actually happened on that eventful day in the Pensacola hotel room. God sent a couple of angels to break off the demons that had attached themselves to me. I did not have anyone walk me through my deliverance; there was not any breaking off of generational curses or confessing of specific sins. Although I believe in these methods of deliverance, God in His sovereignty busted the demons of lust, religion and criticism off of me. I have been free ever since. I give the glory to God, but I know that the angels were the ones sent by God to do the work.

There is a story in the New Testament about a woman who had a child that needed deliverance (Mark 7:25-30). Jesus never went to where the child was. He did not interrogate the mother to find out why the child had a demon. Jesus did not have to hear about the specifics. He simply told the woman to go home for her child had been delivered. Who delivered the child? Jesus was not with the child and my guess is there was not anyone in ministry there either. Or was there? Maybe a few ministering angels had been dispatched to deliver the child.

Can you imagine the kind of ministries forthcoming when God fully initiates His plan? The minister will only need watch as God, through His angels, heals and sets people free. If you are looking for personal credit, this ministry is not for you. When ministering with angels, it will be very obvious that you are not responsible for the results. God is determined to receive all the glory. He will not share it! The angels live and flow in this understanding, and they will not receive the glory either. God gets all the glory.

Many times angels will tell us things that when said will be words of knowledge, words of wisdom or prophecy. This is exactly how the Holy Spirit operates. When an angel is talking to you, the Holy Spirit is talking to you. When an angel leads you to someone in the crowd and gives you something in the spirit to give to them, that is the Holy Spirit in operation.

It is not that the angels are all of a sudden busy working. They have been doing God's bidding all along. This is what they were created to do. We are just beginning to come into an understanding or revelation that it is indeed the angels that are doing the bidding of the Holy Spirit as the Holy Spirit works in this earth.

I know it is easier to relegate angels to their protection functions, but they do more than this. We must see the importance of their ministry in areas such as healing, gifts, anointings, deliverance and spiritual warfare. Whatever they are doing is ordained of the Lord. Following their directions ultimately keeps us in the will of God. For me, this simplifies my part in the ministry.

This level of active interactions with the angels is available to the body of Christ. However, it will not happen in every church. The Lord has taught us that the measure of the angelic within the local body is dependent on how much the leadership in the church is willing to flow in it. God will not have lone rangers nor will He have church members operating with His angels who are in any form of rebellion against their church leadership. The angels will not work with anyone operating in rebellion. For this ministry to operate in our churches, the pastor, leaders and elders must be unified and in submission to what God is doing through His angels. God will not have it any other way. The angels flow through the head of the church, through the other leaders and then down into the congregation. The leadership of the local body needs to have instructions before launching into this ministry. One of the mandates God has given us is to help others with this transition.

What if a pastor or leader does not want to flow in the angelic ministry? I am sorry, but it will not happen in your church. The head must be in complete submission to God. The angels will not be released into the congregation until the leadership has submitted to the Lord in this area. A pastor cannot just ask for this anointing in their church without being very personally affected by it. They have to jump into the water before their congregation can.

The angelic ministry just like the Holy Spirit must be welcomed. If the angels are rejected, then the fullness of the Holy Spirit's involvement in your church will be affected. If He is not allowed to come in His fullness, then He is grieved. He will not force His ministry on any church.

What do you do if your pastor or leader does not want anything to do with the angelic? Number one, pray for your leaders. Be patient and do not dare cause any rebellion within your church. God will speak to His shepherds. They will hear from Him and make a choice. The key is that they will have to be able to hear from God. Once they make their decision on whether or not to invite the kingdom of God to come, then you can make your decision. If they decide it is too costly or too absurd, then you will have to ask the Lord if you can move on to a church that is moving in this area.

Be warned, God may require you to stay and pray for your church. We say we would give our lives for the gospel when we really mean we would give our deaths. Will you give up your desire to minister with angels to fulfill God's purposes in your church? Will you willingly sta where He has put you? DO NOT murmur, gossip, complain or try to start a ground swell to influence your pastor. Instead you must be serious enough to pray and fast. The answer to your prayers may take years. You cannot set time limits on God and you cannot help Him out by trying to nudge the process along. Trust me, if this is God's will for your church, He will accomplish it.

Part of the price to be paid for inviting God's kingdom to come is the criticism you will receive. Most people do not like change, and even more do not like talking about the supernatural realm. There will be a significant difference in the power of God manifested in churches that have allowed the Lord to do what He wants in their congregation. Once the kingdom of God starts settling in a church, the pastor and leaders need to inform the congregation as to what is taking place within the spirit realm and instruct them in how to cooperate with the angels. Many in the congregation will feel very uncomfortable when you begin talking openly about the supernatural realm.

Unfortunately, it has been our experience that when you partner with God and His angels, your church will begin having internal problems. The enemy will fight to the death to keep you from moving forward into these new realms of the spirit. You may have best friends or family members who become divided over the direction that your church is taking. Everyone who is lukewarm or not fully committed will either leave the church or remain and cause strife. Inviting God's kingdom to come is not necessarily a way to grow your church. In fact, during the first four years our church lost two-thirds of its members.

You may remember that Jesus lost many of his disciples when He taught them "hard sayings."

"From that time many of his disciples went back, and walked no more with him. Then said Jesus unto the twelve, Will ye also go away?"

-- John 6:66-67

Other examples include Gideon's army, which God pared down from 32,000 to 300 (Judges 7:3, 6), and the disciples waiting in the Upper Room, which dwindled from 500 at the beginning to only 120 on the Day of Pentecost (1 Corinthians 15:6; Acts 1:15).

For us, it has meant having total commitment to the purposes of God. There are no exceptions, we either do it His way or God will not stay. He is doing the building, although most of what He is building cannot be seen with the natural eye. We are only cooperating and agreeing with Him for what He wants to see happen in our church and city. He does everything in His timing. We do not move until He gives the green light. It is slow, much slower than we think it should be. You will either learn patience or give up out of frustration. God is likely to switch gears on you a time or two to see if you are willing to change things. He will have you stop doing something that may be good and beneficial just to see if you will obey. He does not want us to settle into tradition or patterns that cannot be dropped at a moment's notice. He may lift His presence for a season; to see if you will still pursue Him with the same passion you did when His anointing was so thick.

Why does the presence and ministry of angels cause such a disturbance? There are probably several reasons. For one, when the angels come it intensifies the anointing for intercession. If people do not like praying or hearing from the pastor that they should be praying, then there are going to be problems. When the angels come to assist in intercession several things happen. There will be strange noises, loud praying, odd languages and sounds and plenty of unusual physical manifestations. I am not just talking about the shaking variety of manifestations. There are many unsettling things that happen, and you must consider the potential fallout before you invite the kingdom of God to come in its fullness.

Every program, activity, custom and tradition must be submitted to the chopping block of God. For example, the Lord may tell you to cancel a favorite program, remove hymnals or perhaps the organ. God is not nearly as attached to these things as we are. Our church has removed the organ but not the hymnals. The point is we need to open up to new songs from the Lord.

The cuts can go very deep. The Lord may move leaders and members out of your church. When you hear complaints from the people, will you still obey the voice of the Lord? He will not have people hanging around that make light of or criticize what He is doing.

We would never have dreamed of the ministry team configurations the Lord has put together. Today, our worship team has many teenagers on it. Can your congregation dance? Do they have freedom to prophesy? Does God have permission to do anything He wants in your church?

These things do not mean God 's kingdom has come. So do not try to get God to come by removing hymnals and starting a dance team. God knows and will put His finger on those areas that are hindering your congregation from truly saying and meaning "Whatever you ask God, I will do!"

Have many hours been spent organizing and shaping programs to fit your congregation? Are these programs non-negotiable? Man's reasoning has birthed most of the programs within our churches. God is asking us to consider shelving our ways and plans and adopting His ways. This may seem impossible. If you are a leader, you need to pray and ask God if your church can make this transformation. God does not want us to tinker with the programs and structures of our churches. He wants to eliminate them and start over. Can a church survive this process? Only if they are committed to the purposes of God. I could never again be part of a church that does not have this kind of commitment. What is the purpose of every church? To see "His kingdom come and His will be done." We have prayed for it long enough, now let us step into His kingdom.

In time, the angels will be influencing the worship, preaching, evangelizing, and bringing of miracles. The Lord is removing the veil from our eyes. Will you be one who has the privilege of partnering with God to see phenomenal things happen?

Will you minister with angels?

> *"He that hath an ear, let him hear what the Spirit saith unto the churches."*
>
> *-- Revelation 3:22*

60290763R00079

Made in the USA
Lexington, KY
01 February 2017